BOUND FOR GLORY

BOUND FOR GLORY

1910–1930

FROM THE GREAT MIGRATION
TO THE HARLEM RENAISSANCE

Kerry Candaele

CHELSEA HOUSE PUBLISHERS
Philadelphia

ON THE COVER A mother and son rest on their journey from Florida, joining millions of African Americans who abandoned the racism and poverty of the South for the hope of a more promising future up north.

FRONTISPIECE An entire family packs up its belongings and heads north. Many followed the prospects held out by northern industrialists, who needed workers when World War I stopped the flow of immigrants—a ready supply of cheap labor—from Europe.

Chelsea House Publishers
Editorial Director   Richard Rennert
Production Manager   Pamela Loos
Art Director   Sara Davis
Picture Editor   Judy Hasday

Milestones in Black American History
Series Originator and Adviser   Benjamin I. Cohen
Series Consultants   Clayborne Carson, Darlene Clark Hine

Staff for BOUND FOR GLORY
Senior Editors   Marian Taylor, Jane Shumate
Associate Editor   Therese De Angelis
Editorial Assistant   Kristine Brennan
Senior Designer   Cambraia Magalhães
Picture Researcher   Matthew Dudley

First Printing

1 3 5 7 9 8 6 4 2

Library of Congress Cataloging-in-Publication Data

Candaele, Kerry.
    Bound for Glory: from the great migration to the Harlem renaissance, 1910-1930 / Kerry Candaele.
    p. cm. — (Milestones in Black American history)
Includes bibliographical references (p.) and index.
    ISBN 0-7910-2261-7
    ISBN 0-7910-2687-6 (pbk.)
1. Afro-Americans—History—1877-1964—Juvenile literature. 2. Harlem (New York, N.Y.)—Intellectual life—20th century—Juvenile literature. 3. Afro-Americans—Migrations—Juvenile literature. 4. Harlem Renaissance—Juvenile literature.
I. Title. II. Series.
E185.6.C26.1996
973'.0496—dc20
                                                            95-24514
                                                            CIP
                                                            AC

CONTENTS

MILESTONES IN BLACK AMERICAN HISTORY

INTRODUCTION

In 1913 African Americans throughout the nation celebrated the 50th anniversary of President Lincoln's Emancipation Proclamation. In a poem written to commemorate the occasion, James Weldon Johnson expressed the black community's hopes for the next half century:

> Courage! Look out, beyond, and see
> The far horizon's beckoning span!
> Faith in your God-known destiny!
> We are a part of some great plan.

Optimistic and determined, African Americans began to chart a new course for themselves, demonstrating in numerous ways that they would resist oppression.

Between 1910 and 1930, a deep loathing for the segregation and racial violence of the South prompted more than one million African Americans to heed the radical *Chicago Defender's* call to "leave that benighted land" and migrate north. Northerners recruiting workers for their booming industries offered enticing economic incentives, but the promise of a more progressive atmosphere with better chances for educational and cultural advancement was often motivation enough. The movement continued to gain momentum as those who had migrated wrote glowing reports of the North to the friends and relatives they had left behind.

This mass exodus represented a turning point in southern affairs, providing evidence that unprecedented numbers of blacks would no longer comply with the racist system. It also cast a sharp light on the crucial contributions that African Americans made to the southern economy. Frightened of losing their vital labor force, some southerners raised wages, but many more used coercion to prevent blacks from leaving; a Louisiana lawmaker even tried to make black migration illegal.

Besides deeply affecting the South, the Great Migration permanently altered the landscape of the North. African-American communities within northern cities expanded rapidly, with Chicago's black population doubling and Detroit's increasing sixfold between 1910 and 1920. Migrants enriched these areas with their talents and cultures, and while the adjustment to an urban environment was not easy, many new black residents eagerly seized opportunities. A Mississippi woman named Lillian Harris, for example, brought with her a love of cooking and in New York turned her talent into a business in southern foods that eventually made her one of New York's wealthiest black women. And William Lewis Bulkley, who had been born a South Carolina slave, in 1909 became the first black principal of a largely white New York school.

Such progress frequently met with resistance, however. While racism was generally more subtle in the North, it did exist; housing was segregated, and African Americans were usually consigned to menial jobs, with labor unions unwilling to admit them. The United States military, which was supposedly fighting for democracy around the world since entering World War I in 1917, also practiced discrimination despite the heroism displayed by the 42,000 African-American soldiers who saw combat—heroism readily honored by nations such as France.

Indeed racial tensions during and after World War I were high throughout the United States. Race riots spread like wildfire in the "Red Summer" of 1919, a most notorious case being when the drowning of a black boy in Chicago triggered 13 days of violence in which 38 people were killed. And a revitalized Ku Klux Klan—claiming about four million members—set in motion a wave of terrorism and lynchings.

The new generation of black leaders vigorously opposed such racism and, unlike some of their predecessors, advocated active resistance. W. E. B. Du Bois, cofounder of the National Association for the Advancement of Colored People (NAACP) and editor of its influential journal, had warned black veterans returning from the war that it would be necessary to "marshal every ounce of . . . brain and brawn to fight a sterner, longer, more unbending battle" for true democracy on the home front. With a new women's organization called the Anti-Lynching Crusaders, the NAACP led the fight, publicizing the brutality of lynchings, lobbying for civil rights legislation, and battling for equality in the judicial system. Others followed more radical strategies to confront the nation's entrenched racism: socialist labor leader A. Philip Randolph agitated for economic benefits for the black working class and advocated fighting violence with violence; Jamaican-born Marcus Garvey organized the United Negro Improvement Association to promote the concept of a black racial identity worldwide and to solidify that identity with a future black nation.

Indeed the notion of black pride became the rallying cry of the 1920s, during which many African Americans made deep impressions on the nation's culture. In sports, for example, long jumper William DeHart won a gold medal in the 1924 Olympics; the Harlem Globetrotters first began to dazzle audiences with their skill and humor in 1927; and, perhaps most significantly, in 1920 the Negro Leagues were formed, showcasing some of baseball's finest players, such as Leroy "Satchel" Paige. In the field of entertainment, African-American creative and business genius Oscar Micheaux astounded Hollywood by writing, directing, editing, and distributing 46 films. And in 1926 Carter G. Woodson broadened the scope of the nation's education with the first Negro History Week, an annual event that was expanded to Black History Month in the 1960s.

This cultural advancement reached its zenith in the Harlem Renaissance. Blacks from all over the country flocked to the two-square-mile neighborhood that became a city within New York City, a community in which African Americans felt liberated from the scrutiny of white America, and which soon became home to the best of black American cultural achievement. Art, literature, and music blossomed with the gathering of such talents as Langston Hughes, Zora Neale Hurston, Bessie Smith, and Louis Armstrong. These artists burst upon the national consciousness eloquently expressing, in Hughes's words, their "individual dark-skinned selves without fear or shame." And the popular explosion of African-American jazz music—

which had been born in New Orleans several decades earlier and traveled, evolving, to New York nightclubs—earned the 1920s the nickname the Jazz Age.

The Great Depression, triggered by the 1929 stock-market crash, plunged the nation into economic ruin and ended this incredible surge of creative energy. African Americans were hardest hit by the Depression, with 50 to 60 percent of the black population in many major cities out of work. The Harlem Renaissance dissolved, its artists compelled to find what work they could, where they could. The need to survive supplanted the need to create, even the need to forge a racial identity.

But African Americans had witnessed the greatness they could accomplish. The horizon was indeed far off, as James Weldon Johnson had foretold in his 1913 poem, but by 1930 African Americans had taken strong steps toward this horizon—toward a vision of their cultural, economic, and political possibilities—and they could not turn back.

MILESTONES
1910-1930

1910
- Thousands of southern black men and women begin migrating to northern cities in search of a less racist society with greater economic opportunities. Between 1910 and 1920, Chicago's African-American population will more than double, Cleveland's will quadruple, and Detroit's will increase sixfold.
- Black scholar W. E. B. Du Bois cofounds the National Association for the Advancement of Colored People (NAACP) and edits its influential journal, the *Crisis*.
- Boxer Jack Johnson defeats "white hope" Jim Jeffries to remain world heavyweight champion.

1911
- Black realtor Philip A. Payton begins renting Harlem apartments to African Americans. With whites fleeing the area, the two-square-mile neighborhood becomes a black cultural mecca, attracting both artists and migrants from all over the United States.

1914
- When World War I prevents Europeans from emigrating to America, northern industrialists recruit black southerners to ease labor shortages.
- Jamaican Marcus Garvey organizes the Universal Negro Improvement Association (UNIA) to promote worldwide black nationalism.
- Sam Lucas is cast in the title role of *Uncle Tom's Cabin*, becoming the first black actor to play a leading role in a full-length Hollywood film. Black actors slowly replace white actors in blackface, but African Americans are still depicted stereotypically.

1915
- Educator Booker T. Washington, the era's foremost African-American leader, dies. The new generation of black leaders abandons Washington's accommodationist position for more radical activism.

1917
- A labor dispute in East St. Louis, Missouri, escalates into race riots, with white mobs attacking black neighborhoods. President Woodrow Wilson refuses to send troops to control the violence, which leaves 39 blacks dead and hundreds injured.

• After the United States enters World War I, more than 360,000 blacks enlist and 42,000 see combat.

1918

• New York's all-black 369th Infantry Division battles the Germans on the front lines and never loses ground during the rest of the war. The French government awards the entire division the Croix de Guerre for bravery in action.

• Corporal Freddie Stowers of Illinois's 371st Infantry Regiment is recommended for the Congressional Medal of Honor but is told by officials that his award has been "misplaced"; the United States finally recognizes his achievement posthumously in 1991.

1919

• During the "Red Summer," race riots ignite across the country; the deadliest is in Chicago, where 15 whites and 23 blacks die and more than 500 people are injured.

• The Ku Klux Klan experiences a resurgence in membership—numbering more than four million at its peak—and initiates a wave of lynchings, specifically targeting black veterans. The NAACP, the Anti-Lynching Crusaders, and other activist groups publicize the brutal crimes and agitate for antilynching legislation.

• The UNIA launches the Negro Factories Corporation, which offers loans to independent black businesses and opens a chain of black-owned grocery stores, restaurants, and laundries.

1920

• On the maiden voyage of the *Frederick Douglass*, flagship of the UNIA's Black Star Line, the ship arrives in Havana, Cuba, but fails to make a profit because of a local longshoremen's strike. The shipping line flounders, fueling criticism of Marcus Garvey.

• Oscar Micheaux begins his 30-year-long career of writing, directing, editing, and distributing black films.

• Andrew "Rube" Foster organizes independent black professional baseball teams into the Negro National League.

1922

• Garvey meets with Ku Klux Klan leader Edward Young Clark to solicit funds for the settlement of American blacks in Africa; outraged, many African-American leaders turn against Garvey.

1923

• Marcus Garvey is convicted of mail fraud in connection with Black Star Line advertisements; he will serve time in jail from 1925 to 1927, then be deported to Jamaica.

1925
- A. Philip Randolph establishes the Brotherhood of Sleeping Car Porters, a union that pushes for better wages and working conditions for black railroad workers.
- In the heyday of the Harlem Renaissance, *Survey Graphic* magazine, edited by Alain Locke, devotes an entire issue to the new generation of African-American writers; the periodical's special edition is reissued as the book *The New Negro*.

1929
- The stock market crashes, plunging the nation into the Great Depression. African Americans are particularly hard hit by unemployment; in this time of economic devastation, Harlem's golden era of opportunity comes to an abrupt end.

1

THE GREAT MIGRATION

Farewell—We're Good and Gone" read the signs on the trains. These words were also on the lips of more than a million black southerners who had set out on one of America's most important mass movements. Part of a well-known poem, the words captured the dreams, the poignant memories, and the grand hopes of the men and women who, between the turn of the century and 1930, migrated from the South's countryside to the cities in the North.

Simple enough in its sentiments, the "farewell" was never as easy and the final destination never as sweet as the visions in people's minds. For the Great Migration, as it came to be called, was more than a simple journey for southern blacks. In the North, they hoped to find not merely better jobs but a new sense of citizenship and a new respect for themselves, their families, and their people.

One man who wrote to his southern relatives from Philadelphia, Pennsylvania, captured his initial delight in the change of scene. "I don't have to 'master'

Belongings packed, a sharecropper family prepares to leave its lifelong home. In the century's first 30 years, more than one million southern blacks journeyed to the "Promised Land."

every little boy comes along," he wrote, and "I haven't heard a white man call a colored a nigger . . . since I been in the state of Pa. I can ride in the electric street and steam cars where I get a seat. I don't care to mix with white what I mean I am not crazy about being with white folks, but if I have to pay the same fare I have learn to want the same accommodation."

Similar sentiments were echoed by the thousands of other rural blacks who traveled to Detroit, Chicago, New York, Pittsburgh, and other major northern cities. There, far from the world they had known all their lives, these southerners learned to vote and to express their political, intellectual, and cultural ambitions. The racism and discrimination they knew all too well did not, of course, disappear simply with the act of geographical relocation. But compared to the South they had left behind, the North did indeed look like the promised land.

In 1910 America, the North and South might have been mistaken for two different countries. Isolated and economically backward, the southern states had fewer schools and higher rates of illiteracy than other sections of the country. Nor did most southern cities and towns boast the cultural attractions and distractions of their northern counterparts. Quoted in a 1910 issue of *New York Age* magazine, a former tenant farmer explained why he had left the South: "I didn't want to remain in one little place all my days. I wanted to get out and see something of the world." A black shoemaker interviewed about the same time said he felt "choked" by the "narrow and petty life" he had led in a small Virginia town before he moved to New York City.

Thousands of others simply wanted to flee the menacing racism of the South. Racial segregation (called Jim Crow after a term used in 19th-century minstrel shows) was the norm, and blacks were restricted to "colored" facilities—separate rest rooms, theater and courtroom seats, hospitals, beaches, drinking fountains, schools—most of them vastly inferior to those marked "white." Black southerners were politically powerless, barred from voting booths and elective offices by whites who regularly used violence to keep them in their "place." From the last decade of the 19th century through the first of the 20th century, more black people were lynched (murdered by mobs) than in any other period of American history.

Not surprisingly, many blacks escaped the ever-present threat of violence. Edward A. Johnson, a North Carolina educator and politician, came north, he said, because he could not tolerate the racial violence one day longer. George Henry White told the New York *Daily Tribune* in 1900 that he moved from North Carolina because he "couldn't live there and be a man and be treated like a man." Even prominent black leader Booker T. Washington, who encouraged African Americans to stay in the South and improve it, admitted in a 1903 speech that "for every lynching that takes place . . . a score of colored people leave . . . for the city."

Other forces also drew black people away from the rural South. New farm machinery, which performed the field work that had once been done by hand, pushed thousands of poor tenant farmers off the land and toward the city. In 1915 a severe boll weevil infestation destroyed millions of acres of cotton along with the jobs of those who raised it. A popular folk song summed up the desperate conditions:

> Boll-weevil in de cotton,
> Cut worm in de corn,
> Debil in de white man,
> We's goin' on.

New machinery and the boll weevil provided the push, and World War I provided the pull. In 1914,

African Americans plant peanuts in time-honored style. The post–World War I spread of mechanized farming reduced the need for such labor, driving thousands of agricultural workers out of the South.

when the war's outbreak prevented European laborers from emigrating to the United States, northern industrialists turned to the South for workers. African Americans were happy to oblige.

To recruit employees, northern industries often sent labor agents to the South. These scouts received a fee for every worker they pulled in, making many agents wealthy men. In 1916, Pennsylvania Railroad agents signed up some 12,000 black men as unskilled laborers. Recruiting in the South was usually not a difficult task; some agents simply entered black neighborhoods and posted notices that read, "Anybody want to go to Chicago, see me." There was never a shortage of volunteers.

Some agents proved unscrupulous, promising laborers short hours and high wages for jobs that were actually backbreaking and poorly paid. Others insisted that would-be laborers, especially women, sign harsh and unfair labor contracts. Around 1900, for example, a domestic-help agency in Richmond, Virginia, required prospective maids and cooks to sign this agreement:

> In consideration of my expenses being paid from Richmond to_____and a situation provided for me, I agree to give_____services after arrival as_____ to party or persons paying my expenses. And I further agree that all my personal effects may be subject to their order until I have fulfilled that contract, forfeiting all claims to said personal effects after sixty days after this date should I fail to comply with agreement.

For those considering the North, the most trustworthy information came in the mail. People who received letters from relatives and friends in the North passed them around, sometimes to their pastors, who often read them in church. Judging from surviving correspondence, most of these letters expressed great optimism. A Mississippi carpenter who moved to Chicago, for example, wrote these lines to his family: "I was promoted on the first of the month. I should have been here 20 years ago. I just began to feel like a man. My children are going to the same school with the whites and I don't have to umble to no one. I have registered, will vote the next election and there isn't any 'yes sir' and 'no sir'—its all yea and no and Sam and Bill." Such letters created what some observers called a "moving fever."

Newspaper magnate Robert Abbott made a fortune with his Chicago Defender.

The African-American press, especially the *Chicago Defender*, also encouraged many southern blacks to go north. Founded in 1905 by African-American publisher and editor Robert Abbott, the *Defender* was a radical paper that boldly defended black American interests. The paper was not only read in Chicago but circulated nationally. It was usually passed from hand to hand in the South, where every copy had an estimated 10 black readers.

The *Defender*'s editorial voice was demanding, proud, assertive—and self-consciously northern. "I beg of you, my brothers," one editorial read, "to leave that benighted land." Another claimed that "your leaders will tell you the South is the best place for you. Turn a deaf ear to the scoundrel, and let him stay." The paper also published job advertisements: "Wanted: men for laborers and semi-skilled occupation. Address or apply to the employment department. Westinghouse Electric & Manufacturing Co." The *Defender*, along with Boston's *Guardian* and other northern black papers, persuaded countless readers to come north and discover another world.

And a new world it was, created by people driven to escape persecution, better themselves economically, or simply to leave a boring life or an unhappy family situation. Not surprisingly, the Great Migration transformed the South as well. African-American civil rights spokesman W. E. B. Du Bois regarded the mass movement as the end of the South's old order of black oppression and black compliance with racism. That system was "passing away," Du Bois wrote, "just as surely as the old type of southern gentleman is passing."

Those "southern gentlemen," especially the planters who depended on the labor of black workers, took a bleak view of the Great Migration. "I do not know how the South could live without negro labor," wailed a Georgia plantation owner. "It is the life of the South; it is the foundation of its prosperity. . . . God pity the day when the negro leaves the South."

Progressive southern employers tried to halt the migration by promising blacks better pay and improved treatment. But other planters tried to keep black workers by coercion. One Louisiana lawmaker, for example, introduced a bill that would flatly "prohibit members of the [black] race from going north." Vigilantes sometimes boarded northbound trains to attack black men and women and forcibly return them to their towns of origin.

Southerners found the *Chicago Defender*'s efforts to promote migration so offensive that several cities tried to ban the paper outright. When white-owned southern newspapers asserted that black people were freezing and starving to death in the North, the *Defender* responded tartly. "If you can freeze to death in the North and be free," it asked, "why freeze to death in the South and be a slave, where your mother, sister, and daughter are raped . . . where your father, brother, and son are . . . hung to a pole [and] riddled with bullets?"

The *Defender*'s arguments swept the field. From 1916 to 1918 alone, some 400,000 blacks left the South. Between 1910 and 1920, Chicago's African-American population more than doubled, Cleveland's quadrupled, and Detroit's increased sixfold. Some southern towns lost almost their entire black populations; "Ain't enough people I know left," lamented one woman, "to give me a decent funeral." Meanwhile, blacks found the large northern cities—notably New York, Chicago, Detroit, and Pittsburgh—strange, hostile places, where life, especially at night, was often "wicked" and "fast."

Despite the North's better economic climate, most African Americans who worked there held menial jobs. Labor unions—organizations designed to obtain better work conditions for their members—usually excluded blacks, and many employers simply refused to hire them. Most often, new arrivals could land only the economy's fringe jobs: janitor, elevator operator, domestic, and unskilled laborer.

Some, however, achieved more than they had dared to hope for. William Lewis Bulkley, for example, was born a slave in South Carolina and

became a New York City elementary school principal. In 1909, he was named principal of a predominantly white New York school, thereby becoming the first black person to hold that position. North Carolinian George Henry White, after serving in Congress from 1897 to 1901, moved to Philadelphia after his home state effectively disenfranchised black voters. White became a banker, then founded an all-black community in New Jersey. In northern cities after the Great Migration, the black community's most prominent members were often former southerners.

Black women who left their southern homes for the North often found domestic positions their only option.

Hungry customers, most of them transported southerners, await service at an African-American restaurant in Cleveland, Ohio. The Great Migration introduced northerners to ham hocks, blackeyed peas, chitterlings, and other black southern specialties.

Along with their household goods, southern migrants brought their culture, subtly changing the environment of the northern cities. Restaurants opened with southern-style menus, and southern foods appeared in black-owned groceries. One enterprising southerner, Lillian Harris, later known as Pig Foot Mary, turned her love of cooking into a fortune in New York City.

Born in 1870 in a shanty on the Mississippi Delta, Harris traveled through many northern cities looking for opportunity. In 1901 she moved to New York and began a business in Harlem with a five-dollar investment—three dollars for an old baby carriage and a boiler and two dollars for a batch of pigs' feet. She quickly branched out to other traditional southern foods, including hog maws and chitterlings, which she sold from her traveling restaurant. Her enterprise was fairly successful, and she used her profits to speculate in real estate. By 1917, Harris's keen business sense had made her one of New York's wealthiest black women. Eventually she earned enough to retire to California, where she died in 1929.

But for most migrants, the North was no paradise and no promised land. As in the South, segregation in housing and hiring were the norm, and northern racism sometimes took on a brutality that equaled anything in Mississippi or Alabama. But despite the challenges, most of those who went north never returned to the South, perhaps preferring to forget the place where they had known so much humiliation and suffering. The poet Langston Hughes, himself a Missourian who moved to New York in the 1920s, spoke for many displaced southerners in "One-Way Ticket." Capturing the sense of adventure felt by those who gave up a familiar past for an uncertain future, the poem ends with the following lines:

> I pick up my life
> And take it away
> On a one-way ticket—
> Gone up North,
> Gone out West,
> Gone!

2

SAFE FOR DEMOCRACY?

Published on August 9, 1919, a *New York Age* cartoon contains three figures: a black soldier pointing to a boldly lettered sign, U.S. president Woodrow Wilson looking on intently, and a black sailor holding an American flag. The sign carries this message: "WE FOUGHT TO MAKE THE WORLD SAFE FOR DEMOCRACY AND AMERICA SAFE FOR THE NEGRO."

These words are an angry rejoinder to Wilson's famous assertion that the United States and its allies were fighting World War I to "make the world safe for democracy." Before 1917, Americans had regarded the war, which began in 1914, as a European affair that did not call for U.S. involvement. But the United States had become gradually more involved in the conflict, and in 1917 it finally joined Britain, Russia, France, and Italy against Germany, Austria-Hungary, and the Ottoman Empire (present-day Turkey and the Middle East). Many Americans supported the decision to go to war, but a substantial minority saw no

A 1919 newspaper cartoon illustrates the disappointment of African-American veterans: expecting white acknowledgment of their outstanding war records, they found accelerated racism instead.

27

Dazed residents examine the smoldering remains of their neighborhood after 1917's East St. Louis riots. The rampage left hundreds of blacks dead or injured and thousands more homeless.

obligation or reason for it. For some African Americans, President Wilson's talk of assuring democracy abroad while blacks were denied rights at home seemed like pure hypocrisy.

Only months after the United States entered the war, blacks' absence of guaranteed protection was violently underscored in East St. Louis, Illinois. Large numbers of blacks had recently moved to the city, and local whites feared that the newcomers would flood the labor market. A labor dispute in May sparked the first instance of violence, as white mobs roamed the streets attacking blacks and attempting to force them out of the city. The governor of Illinois called in the National Guard, and a tenuous peace lasted until July, when a group of nervous blacks fired on an approaching car filled with armed whites. The vehicle proved to be a squad car; five policemen were shot, one of them fatally.

The police-car incident confirmed in the minds of white racists the belief that the East St. Louis blacks were a menace that had to be eliminated. White mobs now attacked black neighborhoods, killing 39 residents, injuring hundreds, and driving thousands from their homes.

Throughout the riots, President Wilson refused to send in troops to restore order and save lives. He also failed to condemn the violence publicly. His unwillingness to make even a gesture in defense of the lives, well-being, and property of East St. Louis blacks set off an explosion of protests from African Americans.

Protesting the government's failure to control the East St. Louis riots, African Americans stage a Silent Protest Parade down New York City's Fifth Avenue. At least 30,000 people took part in the demonstration.

In New York City almost 10,000 blacks participated in the Negro Silent Protest Parade, marching wordlessly down Manhattan's Fifth Avenue as another 20,000 people stood watching along the route.

At this point, a professor from Howard University, Kelly Miller, wrote an open letter to Wilson. It said in part, "The Negro, Mr. President, in this emergency, will stand by you and the nation. Will you and the nation stand by the Negro?" Hubert H. Harrison, a black activist who founded the Liberty League of Negro Americans, was even more blunt. "They are saying a great deal about democracy in Washington now," he wrote, "but while they are talking about fighting for freedom and the Stars and Stripes, here at home the whites apply the torch to the black man's homes, and bullets, clubs, and stones to their bodies."

Harrison's point was not lost on other black activists, including the prominent W. E. B. Du Bois. Editor of the *Crisis*, the magazine of the National Association for the Advancement of Colored People (NAACP), Du Bois was also a cofounder of the integrated civil rights organization. "The present war in Europe," Du Bois had asserted in a 1914 *Crisis* editorial, "is one of the great disasters due to race and color prejudice." Du Bois claimed that the conflict was motivated primarily by the European powers' competition to establish colonies in Africa, India, and East Asia.

Regardless of such concerns, when the time came to enlist, African Americans joined the armed forces in large numbers. After the May 1917 passage of the Selective Service Act established the draft, more than two million black Americans registered, 700,000 of them on the first day alone. Ultimately, some 367,000 African Americans entered military service during World War I, and 42,000 saw combat.

Where ordinary black men led, intellectuals soon followed, and by July 1918 Du Bois published "Close Ranks," an editorial in the *Crisis* supporting the war effort. "Let us, while this war lasts," he exhorted, "forget our special grievances and close our ranks shoulder to shoulder with our own white fellow citizens and the allied nations that are fighting for democracy." A month later Du Bois again appealed to his readers' patriotism: "This is our country: We have worked for it, we have suffered for it, we have fought for it." He also expressed the hope that black soldiers' wartime sacrifices would be repaid by postwar gains in the area of civil rights.

An editor, author, and unofficial spokesman for black America, W. E. B. Du Bois originally advised African Americans to disregard World War I. Patriotic blacks, however, enlisted by the tens of thousands, and by mid-1918, Du Bois was cheering them on.

But black civil rights were anything but assured in the military. Under army policy, blacks and whites were trained in separate camps, and initially none of the camps for blacks provided officers' training. After a number of meetings between civil rights activists and military officials, as well as a series of protests by African-American college students, the army began to commission black officers, although in extremely low numbers.

Making matters worse was the case of Lieutenant Colonel Charles Young, the nation's highest-ranking black officer. The son of former Kentucky slaves, Young was a West Point graduate—the third African American so distinguished, he was commissioned as an officer in 1889—who had commanded the 9th Ohio Regiment in Cuba during the 1898 Spanish-

Recruits listen to a Bible lesson at Camp Travis, Texas, during World War I. Throughout the conflict, black servicemen lived and trained in completely segregated facilities.

American War. Promoted to captain, Young had served all over the world, from the Philippines to Haiti to Liberia.

During the 1916 U.S. military campaign against Mexican bandit leader Pancho Villa, Young covered himself with glory as squadron commander of the tough 10th Cavalry under legendary General John "Black Jack" Pershing. Impressed by Young's courage and skill, Pershing secured his promotion to lieutenant colonel. That same year the NAACP awarded its prestigious Spingarn Medal to Young for his outstanding performance as military attaché in Liberia.

Despite Young's extraordinary military record, in the summer of 1917 President Woodrow Wilson found himself swamped with complaints about Colonel Young from white army officers. Their grievances were echoed by several U.S. senators, conspicuously John Sharpe Williams of Mississippi. Young was also the subject of a series of concerned letters between Wilson and Secretary of War Newton D. Baker. Although carefully worded, the objections to Young amounted to little: his white counterparts wanted him out of the army simply because he outranked them and he was black.

Wilson knew he could not order the dismissal of Young, a high-ranking and loyal officer, without stirring up a hornet's nest among blacks and army personnel. On the other hand, the president was eager to placate the powerful southern senators, and he realized, as he wrote Baker on July 3, 1917, that "there is some danger of trouble of a serious nature if this officer [Young] is not separated from his present command." Baker understood his chief. He described the Young situation as "very embarrassing."

Young's medical records showed that he had high blood pressure, giving the War Department a convenient means of getting him out of the way; the colonel was retired from active service in the summer

Colonel Charles Young leaves for a diplomatic assignment in the black African republic of Liberia in 1920. Resentful of Young's high rank in the army, white officers tried to get rid of him, but the fiercely determined trailblazer triumphed in the end.

of 1917. Not surprisingly, the patriotic Young strongly objected to being railroaded out of military service in the middle of a war. Aiming to change the War Department's mind, he decided to prove that he was in good health. On June 6, 1918, he mounted a horse and left Wilberforce, Ohio, for Washington, D.C., a 497-mile trip. Unaccompanied, he made the trek to the capital in 16 days. Young's efforts eventually paid off; although he had to sit out the war, the military recalled him to active service later that year.

Before black soldiers arrived on the European battlefront, they had to fight prejudice and sometimes violence in the camps where they trained. The majority of the white officers placed in command of black soldiers were from the South, and they sometimes made life unbearable for their troops. Blacks at training camps were routinely insulted and given the dirtiest and hardest jobs, and orders from the War Department to rectify such treatment were often ignored. Even more hostile were white southern civilians, who feared that the presence of large numbers of armed northern blacks would threaten the strict racial hierarchy that had traditionally ruled the South. Indeed, southern whites so vigorously opposed the presence of northern black soldiers that the War Department briefly adopted a policy (one that quickly proved impractical) of training blacks only in camps located in their home states.

The conflicts between black soldiers and white civilians rapidly escalated to open violence. When some 600 men of the all-black 24th Infantry Division were assigned to duty in Houston, Texas, they discovered a singularly oppressive atmosphere where racial insults were common, Jim Crow laws the norm, and resentment against black soldiers regularly and openly expressed. Disputes promptly arose between black military policemen (MPs) and local white policemen; in at least two incidents white police officers beat and

arrested unarmed black MPs, and in one case a policeman shot at a black MP who was attempting to escape
his custody.

These attacks outraged members of the 24th division, and in August 1917 some 150 armed black
soldiers entered the city of Houston at night on a
punitive raid against the police. The soldiers killed 17
white men (including five Houston police officers)
before they were overwhelmed by a combined force of
city police, the Texas National Guard, and some
visiting members of the Illinois National Guard.

Of the 156 soldiers court-martialed on charges of
mutiny, 41 were sentenced to life in prison, 13 were
hanged immediately, and 6 were executed at later
dates. The army had alleged, but not proved, that the
riot was not a spontaneous uprising but a carefully
planned plot to disrupt the country in wartime. The
black press saw matters differently; one Baltimore
newspaper asserted that "The Negroes of the entire
country will regard the 13 Negro soldiers of the
Twenty-fourth Infantry executed as martyrs." The
New York Age stated that "strict justice has been done,
but full justice has not been done. . . . And so sure as
there is a God in heaven, at some time in some way
justice will be done."

Despite such incidents, more than 200,000 black
soldiers were sent to Europe during World War I. The
army treated most of them as little more then laborers
in uniform, assigning them to unload ships, haul coal
and stone, clean latrines, and dig ditches. Although
this work was not glamorous, the black soldiers who
did it formed, in the words of one war correspondent,
"a very important cog . . . in the war machinery."

These African Americans accomplished amazing
physical and mental tasks. Working day and night in
all kinds of weather, they established a reputation as
eager and dedicated men. Black stevedores at Bor-
deaux, France, unloaded almost 800,000 tons of ma-

terial in September 1918—an average of 25,000 tons per day. Another work crew at Brest, France, unloaded 1,200 tons of flour in nine and one-half hours. (Far from being exhausted, the crew kept up this back-breaking pace for five more days just to try to beat their own record.) Black work crews often kept up their pace by having a member lead the group in a song with a fast tempo or by having some members act as "jolliers," jokers and storytellers who helped keep the soldiers' spirits high.

The 42,000 African-American soldiers who actually saw combat during World War I performed brilliantly. New York's 369th Infantry Division arrived in France in early 1918. By May these soldiers were fighting in Champagne, France, and in July they positioned themselves in the path of an expected German offensive at Minaucourt. From then until the end of the war the 369th was almost constantly in action against the Germans, at one point remaining in the trenches for 191 days straight.

The Germans dubbed the members of the 369th division the "Hell Fighters," a name they fully deserved, and their own commanding officer, Colonel William Hayward, claimed "my men never retire [retreat]. They go forward or they die." Hayward was not exaggerating; the Hell Fighters never lost a man through capture and never lost ground. After the war, the grateful French government awarded the entire division its most prestigious medal, the Croix de Guerre, and 171 individual division members were given both the Croix de Guerre and the French Legion of Honor.

The all-black 371st Infantry Regiment from Illinois also saw sustained combat in France, remaining on the front lines for more than three months. The French government honored the division enthusiastically, awarding 3 of its officers the Legion of Honor and 34 officers and 89 enlisted men the Croix de Guerre. The United States also recognized the division's gallantry in battle by awarding 14 of its officers and 12 of its enlisted men the Distinguished Service Cross.

But the U.S. government was less forthcoming with its highest award, the Congressional Medal of Honor. Corporal Freddie Stowers of the 371st was recommended for this honor after he led an assault against a German-held outpost at the top of a well-fortified hill. During the charge, Stowers's company lost more than half its men but managed nonetheless to take the outpost. But Stowers, the only black member of the armed forces to be recommended for the Medal of Honor in World War I, never received his award (officials told him it had been "misplaced"). The United States finally granted Stowers his due honors posthumously in 1991.

America's shoddy treatment of its black citizens was no secret in Europe. Racism, in fact, formed the basis for an intense German propaganda campaign aimed at the black soldiers of the 92nd division, also stationed in France. The Germans peppered the division's territory with pamphlets containing some pointed questions for African-American soldiers: "Can you get a seat in the theater where white people sit?" "Is lynching and the most horrible crimes connected therewith a lawful proceeding in a democratic country?" The leaflets invited the blacks to come over to their lines, where they would find true friends who

Supervised by a white officer, black soldiers work on a railway track near Brest, France, during World War I. The U.S. Army used most of its African-American troops as laborers, but those who got to the front lines proved themselves top-notch fighting men.

would help them in their struggle for equality. Despite such temptations, no man of the 92nd ever deserted to the Germans.

The High Command placed some American divisions, a few of them black, under French command, and blacks and French got along well. "Never will the 157th French Division forget," proclaimed French general Mariano Goybet, "the indomitable dash, the heroic rush of the [371st Infantry Regiment] up the observatory ridge and into the plains of Monthois [a battle site in France]. . . . These crack regiments overcame every obstacle with a most complete contempt for danger."

When they came to France, black soldiers brought not only their courage but their culture, and they left behind a musical legacy that has lasted to the present day. The black jazz bands organized to boost the morale of American soldiers became the toast of France. The most famous, the 369th Regiment Band led by Lieutenant James R. Europe, covered 2,000 miles and played in 25 French cities. In later years, many American jazz musicians discovered that their most dedicated and serious audiences lay across the Atlantic.

The French, both military and civilian, associated freely with African-American soldiers. This friendliness disturbed some members of the American High Command, which, in August 1918, issued a document addressed to the "French Military Mission Stationed with the American Army" and captioned "Secret Information Concerning the Black American Troops." The document concluded with these "suggestions":

> 1. We must prevent the rise of any pronounced degree of intimacy between French officers and black officers. We may be courteous and amiable with the last, but we cannot deal with them on the same plane as with the white

OUR COLORED HEROES

American officer without deeply wounding the latter. We must not eat with them, must not shake hands or seek to talk or meet with them outside of the requirements of military service.

2. We must not commend too highly the [black] American troops, particularly in the presence of [white] Americans....

3. Make a point of keeping the native [civilian] population from spoiling the Negroes. [White] Americans become greatly incensed at any public expression of intimacy between white women and black men.

"Our Colored Heroes," a 1918 lithograph, depicts Sergeant Henry Johnson of the 369th Infantry Division, Harlem's famed "Hell Fighters," single-handedly taking on a 36-man German unit. In the action, he killed 4 and captured 32 of the enemy, using a bolo knife when he ran out of ammunition.

Sergeant Henry Johnson of the "Hell Fighters" received France's Croix de Guerre for his bravery.

But the French generally ignored such advice and continued to fraternize with African Americans. Their attitude pleased the black soldiers, many of whom observed that the ideals of democracy seemed a few steps closer in France. When World War I ended in November 1918 with the defeat of Germany, these soldiers hoped to return to a United States that was also nearer to fulfilling its democratic ideals.

Writing at his eloquent and angry best in a May 1919 *Crisis* editorial, W. E. B. Du Bois captured the mood of many African American veterans:

> This is the country to which we Soldiers of Democracy return. This is the fatherland for which we fought! But it

A wounded veteran gets a warm "welcome home" from proud neighbors. After helping achieve liberty in Europe, black soldiers vowed to achieve it in America: "We return from fighting," said W. E. B. Du Bois. "We return fighting."

is *our* fatherland. It was right for us to fight. The faults of *our* country are *our* faults. Under similar circumstances we would fight again. But by the God of Heaven, we are cowards and jackasses if now that that war is over, we do not marshal every ounce of our brain and brawn to fight a sterner, longer, more unbending battle against the forces of hell in our own land.

We *return*.
We *return from fighting*.
We *return fighting*.
Make way for Democracy! We saved it in France, and by the Great Jehovah, we will save it in the United States of America, or know the reason why.

3

AFTER THE WAR

When the veterans returned from war in late 1918 and early 1919, America was the scene of sharp contrasts. The nation was entering the "Roaring Twenties," a period of booming prosperity; at the same time, it was bleeding from the multiple wounds of racial violence. From June 1919 to the end of that year—a time tagged the "Red Summer" by NAACP chief James Weldon Johnson—race riots blazed across the country, leaving scores dead and thousands injured.

Postwar America sometimes resembled a series of war zones, with whites attacking black neighborhoods and blacks fighting back and—when they could—launching counterattacks. The deadliest of these disturbances occurred in July 1919 in Chicago, where the drowning of a black boy touched off 13 days of mayhem in which 38 people died and 537 suffered injury. Much of the antiblack violence was spontaneous, but some of it was organized. When African-American veterans returned from fighting the Germans, they confronted another hostile, uniformed army: the white-skinned, white-robed Ku Klux Klan (KKK). Founded after the Civil War to destroy southern

Passing an arch that welcomes returning troops, the legendary 369th Division thunders up New York City's Fifth Avenue. In celebrating the war's victorious finale, white America lavished honors on black veterans, but the sense of brotherhood proved short-lived.

A crowd of Chicagoans—many of them children—cheer as smoke billows from a black residence they have just torched. The ghoulish scene took place during the race riots that rocked the midwestern city in the summer of 1919.

blacks' political strength, the Klan had changed slightly by the 1920s. It still offered a message of bigotry, violence, and bitter hatred of black people, but now its list of enemies included Jews, Catholics, atheists, immigrants, and anyone else racially or morally "impure."

During its heyday in the mid-1920s, the Klan claimed a membership of more than four million. Its political influence extended across much of the country, and its monthly income exceeded $40,000. Klan members waged a campaign of terror and violence against "undesirables"; costumed in white hoods and sheets, they burned crosses near their targets' homes and kidnapped, beat, and even murdered those they had judged "guilty" of some "crime"—usually while local law enforcers looked the other way.

Black veterans galled Klan members most of all. Their confidence strengthened by experience in war, black men with military training could, by KKK standards, be nothing but trouble. Of the more than 70 blacks reported lynched in 1919, 10 were soldiers. These lynchings were particularly gruesome. The killers drenched 14 of the victims with gasoline and burned them publicly; 11 were alive when the match touched the fuel.

Pushed to the wall, blacks organized a campaign against lynching, hoping that public horror would lead to legislation against it. Powering the

Holding an American flag and backed by the U.S. Capitol, robed Ku Klux Klan members parade through Washington, D.C. Absurd as they often appeared, these men (and sometimes women) cut a swath of terror through the nation's black communities in the years following World War I.

A mob in Excelsior Springs, Missouri, watches the death throes of Miller Mitchell, a black falsely accused of raping a white woman, in 1925. In this era, the number of lynchings rose to one every other day.

antilynching effort was the vigorous commitment of thousands of African-American women (one of the first of whom had been Ida Wells-Barnett, the crusading journalist who led an almost one-woman antilynching campaign in the 1890s). A group of black women associated with the NAACP and other organizations formed a committee to fight lynching that became known as the Anti-Lynching Crusaders. Led by Mary B. Talbert, a longtime educator and a tireless organizer, the crusaders sent such activists as Grace Nail Johnson and Alice Dunbar Nelson all over the country to speak to church and civic groups, publicizing the extent and barbarity of violence against blacks. As an editor of the journal *Women's Voice* wrote, "The women will begin with prayer at a sunrise, and end with prayer at a sunset—in between they will do much more sweaty work than praying."

Talbert also sought the support of white women's organizations. As most of these groups viewed lynching as a "black issue" instead of a "women's issue," this work required an especially energetic approach. White women did eventually establish the Association of Southern Women for the Prevention of Lynching, but the leadership of the antilynching movement remained in black hands.

One set of these hands belonged to educator Mary McLeod Bethune. Born in Mayesville, South Carolina, the 15th of 17 children, Bethune trained to become a teacher and a missionary. She originally intended to work abroad but decided instead to establish a school for girls in Daytona, Florida. Raising money by selling pies and cakes, in 1904 Bethune founded the Daytona Normal and Industrial Institute for Negro Girls, later called Bethune-Cookman College.

Bethune's enthusiasm and eloquence soon won her an influential position among black female activists. In 1917 she became president of the Florida Federation of Colored Women, a post she held until 1924, when she became president of the National Association of Colored Women. In 1920 she founded and headed the Southeastern Federation of Colored Women, a regional association of black women's groups. By this point a public figure, Bethune met a number of important political figures, including the governor of New York, Franklin Delano Roosevelt, in

1927. Bethune and the governor's wife, Eleanor Roosevelt, became fast friends, and in 1935, Franklin Roosevelt, by then president of the United States, named Bethune head of the National Youth Administration's Division of Negro Affairs. The appointment made her the first black woman to serve as a federal agency chief.

Black women were not alone in the fight against lynching. Because local and state authorities rarely punished the crime, one of the Anti-Lynching Crusaders' major goals was the passage of legislation that would make lynching a federal crime, an objective the Crusaders shared with the NAACP. By the early 1920s, these crusaders had persuaded Congress to introduce an antilynching bill. Southern senators defeated it, as they did every such measure ever proposed to Congress.

Mary McLeod Bethune shares a laugh with her friend and supporter, First Lady Eleanor Roosevelt, at a National Youth Administration (NYA) conference in Washington, D.C. President Franklin Roosevelt's appointment of Bethune as chief of the NYA's Division of Negro Affairs made her the first black woman to run a federal agency.

But the antilynching campaigns did have an effect. An estimated 300 lynchings took place between 1919 and 1923, but between 1924 and 1928 the number dropped to 100. Contributing heavily to this decline were the educational efforts of the Crusaders and the NAACP, both of which publicized photographs, eyewitness reports, and statistics that demonstrated the viciousness of the crime.

Before the two organizations began their campaigns, many Americans believed that blacks were lynched to punish them for raping white women. Walter White, successor to NAACP secretary James Weldon Johnson, pointed out in his 1948 memoirs, *A Man Called White*, that "Americans were astounded (some of them still are) to learn that fellow Americans have been put to death by mobs for such 'crimes' as 'being too prosperous for a Negro,' talking back to a white man, and for refusing to turn out of the road to let a white boy pass." Although the government failed to outlaw lynching, the Crusaders and the NAACP made Americans more aware of it, thereby reducing its incidence.

White was a key figure in the antilynching campaign. Born in Atlanta, Georgia, in 1893, he moved to New York to join the NAACP as an assistant secretary in 1918. Twelve days after his arrival, he and Secretary Johnson learned of the fate of Jim McIlherron. A black Tennessee sharecropper, McIlherron had been slowly burned to death by a mob for defending himself against a beating by his employer. Walter White, who was blond, fair skinned, and blue eyed, had never before even considered passing for a white man, but now he decided to do so in order to investigate McIlherron's murder.

Posing as a white businessman, White traveled to Tennessee, where he soon uncovered the gruesome details of the crime. As he recorded in *A Man Called White*:

The first few times the conversation veered toward the lynching I purposely exhibited eagerness to talk about politics or the weather or cotton-raising. My studied indifference and apparent ignorance of the fact that there had been any trouble began to become highly irritating to [local farmers]. Even when they boasted and began to reveal far more than they realized as to the actual participants I deliberately intimated that I had known of much more exciting lynchings than that of McIlherron. When local pride had thus been sufficiently disparaged, the facts came tumbling forth. It was difficult to suppress evidence of my anger and nausea at the gruesome recital. The white man who had beaten McIlherron had no just cause for doing so, they admitted, and he was universally distrusted and disliked in the community. When I asked why then they had taken such terrible vengeance on McIlherron for refusing to submit to undeserved mistreatment from such a man, I was told "any time a nigger hits a white man, he's gotta be handled or else all the niggers will get out of hand."

When White returned to New York, the NAACP published the facts and details of the McIlherron lynching, which created a sensation—especially when the lynchers realized, as White put it, that he was "a Negro who had been housed and fed in their local hotel." White continued to investigate lynchings in the South, often at considerable risk to his own life.

For example, during a 1919 visit to Arkansas, where he was checking out a case in which 12 innocent black sharecroppers were about to be hanged, White was tipped off that the local whites had discovered he was a black NAACP investigator. He raced aboard a departing train, where a chatty conductor told him he was making a mistake in departing the area. "You're leaving, mister, just when the fun is going to start," he said. "There's a damned yellow nigger down here passing for white and the boys are going to get him."

"What'll they do with him?" White asked.

"When they get through with him," the grinning conductor assured him, "he won't pass for white no more!"

Safely back at NAACP headquarters, White wrote an extensive report about the unjustly accused sharecroppers. His revelations sparked an outpouring of public support, enabling the NAACP to keep the case open. Four years later, White and his organization managed to get the Arkansas decision reviewed by the U.S. Supreme Court, which eventually cleared all 12 condemned men.

Another tireless NAACP antilynching worker was the association's director of publicity and research, W. E. B. Du Bois. A prominent scholar long before he helped establish the NAACP, Du Bois had gained national recognition in 1903, when he published his book *The Souls of Black Folk: Essays and Sketches*. Among his many contributions to the NAACP was the creation of its monthly magazine, the *Crisis*, which he edited until 1934.

Du Bois used the pages of the *Crisis* to champion black freedom and women's rights, to condemn anti-Semitism and European colonialism, and to challenge capitalism and the status quo. With his graceful, scholarly style, Du Bois became highly regarded among readers of all races. Indeed, as historian Manning Marable has noted, by the 1920s Du Bois had become an "institution," in much the same manner that Frederick Douglass, the great 19th-century black abolitionist, had become a hero and spokesman for his generation.

But to white racists, Du Bois was hardly a hero. The governor of Mississippi, for example, offered a thinly veiled threat when he invited Du Bois to his state, promising to make him an "example . . . that would be a lasting benefit to the colored people of the South." A Dallas newspaper ran a front-page editorial in 1923 proclaiming that "the arrogant ebony-head, thick-lipped, kinky-haired Negro 'educator' must be put in his place and made to stay there."

Du Bois seemed impervious to criticism, even when it came from some of the NAACP's conservative white members. When a board member criticized the *Crisis's* strong antilynching position in 1914, Du Bois defended his editorial policy and ended up gaining complete control of the magazine's contents. (During his tenure as *Crisis* editor, Du Bois edited or wrote all or part of 19 books—a fraction of his prodigious lifetime literary and scholarly output.) His editorials, reviews, and articles reveal a man of great moral courage who stood fast in the face of adversity.

Du Bois's unyielding nature did not make him easy to work with, and he publicly feuded with dozens of black leaders, including Booker T. Washington, Marcus Garvey, and Walter White. But some of the NAACP's opposition would probably have existed even without Du Bois. Many of the organization's black members were prosperous, college educated, and conspicuously light skinned, qualifications that made them less than sympathetic to working-class African Americans. Furthermore, wealthy white philanthropists played a major role in establishing the organization, encouraging the notion that it was basically an exclusive club for snobs. Some blacks even mockingly called it the "National Organization for the Advancement of *Certain* People."

During the early 1920s, two of the most outspoken critics of Du Bois and the NAACP were A. Philip Randolph and Chandler Owen. Both unyielding so-

cialists, the two men edited the *Messenger*, a vigorous monthly journal that called itself "The Only Radical Negro Magazine in America." According to Randolph and Owen, the NAACP's stress on court cases and legislation made it almost irrelevant to most black Americans, who cared more about putting food on the table than about gaining technical legal rights. "The NAACP is led, controlled and dominated by a group," claimed the *Messenger*, "who are neither Negroes nor working people, which renders it utterly impossible to articulate the aims of a group that are the victims of certain social, political and economic evils as a race, and as a part of the great working people."

Unlike NAACP leaders, Randolph and Owen encouraged black Americans to fight violence with violence. "A bullet," sternly observed a 1919 *Messenger* editorial, "is sometimes more convincing than a hundred prayers, editorials, sermons, protests, and petitions." But the staunchly socialist *Messenger*'s editors

Labor leader A. Philip Randolph (left) represents the Brotherhood of Sleeping Car Porters in a meeting with Edward Morrow of the Railroad Mediation Board in 1926. A politial radical and NAACP opponent, Randolph started his career as editor of a left-wing magazine, the Messenger.

saw capitalism, not racism, as the black worker's most dangerous enemy. "The employing class," a 1918 editorial asserted, "recognize no race lines. They will exploit a white man as readily as a black man. They will exploit women as readily as men. They will even go to the extent of coining the labor, blood and suffering of children into dollars."

In order to combat employers, said Randolph and Owen, black workers should organize into unions. Unfortunately, however, blacks were more eager to join the unions than the unions were to accept blacks. The American Federation of Labor (AFL), the strongest workers' organization in the 1920s, welcomed white-only unions and never recruited black laborers. Randolph and Owen supported a more egalitarian union organization, the radical International Workers of the World (IWW), but it became a target of massive federal opposition in 1917 and never recovered its earlier prominence.

As her bag-laden porter waits patiently, a passenger makes her leisurely departure from New York City's Penn Station in the 1920s. Until Philip Randolph organized them, railroad porters labored long hours for low pay and little respect.

The *Messenger* itself ran into trouble for its socialist views. In 1919 a New York State committee established to investigate radical groups dubbed the magazine
"the most dangerous of all the Negro publications."
Basing its opinion on the committee's findings, the
U.S. State Department promptly declared Randolph
"the most dangerous Negro in America." Police raided
the magazine's office and briefly jailed the two editors.
Four years later Owen moved to Chicago, leaving
Randolph alone in New York with his "dangerous"
magazine, dwindling funds, and no solution to the
racism that excluded blacks from unions.

Still undaunted in 1925, Randolph agreed to help
unionize the African-American porters and maids of
the Pullman Company, owner and operator of the
nation's railroad sleeping cars. Organizing these employees was no small feat in the face of implacable
opposition from the wealthy company; it took Randolph, in fact, more than a decade to force Pullman
to recognize and negotiate with his union. Randolph's
efforts not only improved the lives of Pullman's maids
and porters but helped lower the color barrier that
excluded blacks from established unions.

Despite their differences, the black activists of the
early 20th century had one thing in common: they
were far more willing to complain about racism than
their predecessors. Led by educator Booker T. Washington (who died in 1915), the older black generation
had advocated meeting racism with compliance and
moderation—a strategy scornfully called "Old Negro"
by militant activists. "The Old Negro and his futile
methods must go," wrote Cyril V. Briggs, leader of the
black nationalist African Blood Brotherhood. "His
abject crawling and pleading have availed the Cause
nothing." The emergence of the "New Negro"—a
black person who took pride in his or her race, culture,
and color—became the black rallying cry of the 1920s.

4

MARCUS GARVEY AND PAN-AFRICANISM

R ace pride" became the password for a generation of African Americans. Many of the concept's advocates stirred debate, but the most controversial was Marcus Garvey, the Jamaican-born leader of the United Negro Improvement Association (UNIA). A black nationalist organization that promoted racial honor and self-improvement, the UNIA had more followers than any African-American mass movement in U.S. history. Both the UNIA and its leader would inspire—and enrage—millions.

Marcus Mosiah Garvey was born in 1887 and left Jamaica as a young man to travel and to work. Employed sometimes as a printer but usually as a laborer, he traveled throughout Central America and then Europe. Everywhere he went, he saw that the descendants of Africans were oppressed and treated as second-class citizens, and he resolved that he would change things. While he was living in London, Garvey read Booker T. Washington's 1901 autobiography, *Up from Slavery*, and decided to follow in his footsteps: he, too, would be a full-time activist, and he would lead the world's black people out of bondage. "'Where is the black man's Government?'" he later

Watched by a cheering multitude, a United Negro Improvement Association (UNIA) parade snakes through the streets of Harlem in August 1920. As UNIA leader Marcus Garvey had anticipated, the organization's parade and convention stopped Harlem in its tracks.

Marcus Mosiah Garvey, a man of enormous vision and ambition, saw no end to black America's economic and political future. Unfortunately for him, his dreams outran his diplomatic skills; antagonizing not only the U.S. government but most of the nation's black leadership, Garvey wound up broke, deported, and friendless.

reported asking himself. "'Where is his King and his kingdom?' 'Where is his President, his country, and his ambassador, his army, his navy, his men of big affairs?' I could not find them, and then I declared, 'I will help to make them.'"

In 1914 Garvey returned to Jamaica and founded the UNIA. The organization was based on the philosophy of pan-Africanism, the idea that all people of African descent shared a common problem—racism—and should therefore work toward a common political solution. Because Europeans ignored geographical boundaries, dominating blacks in Africa as well as abroad, Garvey believed that blacks all over the world should join hands to replace national identity with race identity.

Meeting with only limited success in Jamaica, in 1916 Garvey left to raise funds in the United States. After a shaky start, he established a UNIA branch in Harlem and in 1918 began printing the *Negro World*. The weekly paper contained his analysis of current events, detailed descriptions of UNIA proceedings, profiles of black historical leaders, and letters, poetry, and short stories sent in by black readers from around the world. At the peak of its success, the paper boasted a worldwide circulation of 60,000, and it appeared in French, Spanish, and English editions. The *Negro World* attracted the attention not only of black readers but of white authorities, who regarded it as subversive. Its distribution was soon banned in most British and French territories.

But Garvey remained as militant as ever. Unlike the NAACP, the UNIA solicited no support from white philanthropists or white-owned businesses. Nor did it seek to associate itself with any larger political party. Republicans, Democrats, and Socialists "are the same to us," Garvey claimed in a July 1919 issue of *Negro World*. "They are all white men to us and all of them join together and lynch and burn negroes."

Black Americans, disgusted with the white-on-black violence that had swept the country after World War I, flocked to the UNIA. By the middle of 1919, Garvey claimed that the organization had more than two million members and 30 branches worldwide. Blacks were also attracted to Garvey himself; one Harlemite later described him as "a little sawed-off, hammered down black man, with determination written all over his face, and an engaging smile that caught you and compelled you to listen to his story."

A tireless worker, Garvey traveled all over the United States and Canada, often speaking in two places a day to drum up support for his organization. He was a spellbinding orator, enthusiastically recounting the glories of African civilization, decrying black self-hatred, and promoting black self-reliance. One of his favorite phrases —"Up, you mighty race"— became the battle cry of the UNIA.

Emboldened by the UNIA's growing influence and popularity, Garvey called a Harlem convention of UNIA branches and other black organizations in August 1920. The convention, a tremendous success, was crowned by a parade so vast it actually shut down Harlem. Thousands gathered to watch as Garvey, seated in an open automobile and wearing a spectacular uniform and immense plumed hat, rode through the streets in triumph. Also highly visible were the vivid uniforms of the African Legions—a force that Garvey hoped would one day help reclaim Africa from its European occupiers—and 200 white-uniformed Black Cross nurses, who represented the UNIA's commitment to aiding the black community's sick and needy members.

Delegates to the 1920 convention set up a model government for a future black nation. They elected Garvey provisional president of Africa and granted other UNIA officials similarly exalted titles. Critics mocked these elections (the vast majority of the delegates had never been to Africa), but Garvey was not, as some claimed, a deluded would-be emperor. What he

wanted to do—and did—was emphasize the common racial bond among people of African descent and encourage these people to take pride in their roots.

In a 1919 issue of *Negro World*, Garvey had outlined his plan for improving black life: "If we are . . . to become a great national force, we must start business enterprises of our own; we must build ships and start trading with ourselves between America, the West Indies, and Africa." Eager to promote black enterprise, the UNIA established the Negro Factories Corporation, which was to create black-owned businesses throughout the country. The corporation opened and operated a number of concerns, including laundries, restaurants, and a grocery-store chain, and provided loans and guidance to independent black businesses.

Marcus Garvey and the UNIA also began a more ambitious project: the Black Star Line. Conceived as a business venture to speed the liberation of the black race, the line dominated UNIA fund-raising efforts for the next few years. Organizers traveled around the country selling $5-a-share company stock, which was snapped up by eager supporters. Even Du Bois, who was critical of what he considered a utopian and ill-defined scheme, was intrigued. In the January 1921 issue of the *Crisis*, he noted: "What he [Garvey] is trying to say and do is this: American Negroes can be accumulating and ministering their own capital, organize industry, join the black centers of the south Atlantic by commercial enterprise and in this way ultimately redeem Africa as a fit and free home for black men. This is true. It is *feasible*."

Tens of thousands of African Americans, even if they had no intention of leaving the United States for Africa, contributed to Garvey's cause. The lure of the UNIA and the Black Star Line was especially strong

A Harlem sign identifies Garvey's Black Star Corporation, a shipping company that became a rallying point for racial pride. Although the line ultimately failed, black men and women around the globe saw it as proof that they could compete on an international economic scale.

in the American South, the Caribbean, and Latin America, where many poor blacks were proud to feel they had contributed to the redemption of Africa. One Panamanian wrote to Garvey: "I have sent twice to buy shares amounting to $125. . . . Now I am sending $35 for seven more shares. You might think I have money, but the truth, as I have stated before, is that I have no money now. But if I'm to die of hunger it will be all right because I'm determined to do all that's in my power to better the conditions of my race."

Garvey's vision was intoxicating, but the Black Star Line was crucially hampered by Garvey's and other UNIA officials' near-total ignorance of the shipping industry. The first steamship purchased by the Black Star Line, the *Yarmouth* (rechristened the *Frederick Douglass*), was barely seaworthy. When, to the cheers of thousands of Harlemites, the ship embarked in 1919 from Manhattan's 135th Street, she got only as far as 23rd Street, due to a legal disagreement with her previous owner.

The *Douglass's* first voyage was no less troubled. Arriving in Havana, Cuba, the ship was immobilized by a 32-day longshoreman's strike. Because the vessel never made a profitable cargo run, her operation was a drain on UNIA funds. Garvey purchased other ships, but they were as poorly outfitted as the first. The Black Star Line never realized his dreams.

The shipping company's failure embarrassed Garvey and encouraged his critics. Often abrasive and arrogant toward those with whom he disagreed, Garvey acquired a number of enemies among moderate black leaders. His bitterest rival turned out to be Du Bois, who, he claimed in a 1923 *Negro World* article, "bewails every day the drop of Negro blood in his veins" and was the perfect "stooge" for the whites who "actually controlled" the NAACP. Du Bois struck back with equal vehemence in a *Crisis* editorial,

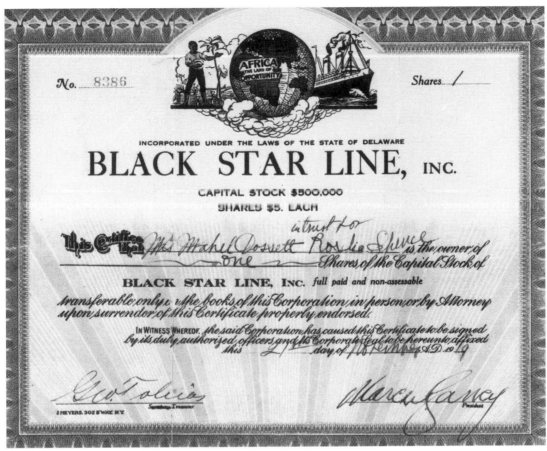

No. 8386   Shares 1

INCORPORATED UNDER THE LAWS OF THE STATE OF DELAWARE

BLACK STAR LINE, INC.

CAPITAL STOCK $500,000
SHARES $5. EACH

This Certifies that Mrs Mabel Dossett *in trust for* Rosalie Shives *is the owner of* ———— one ———— *Shares of the Capital Stock of*

BLACK STAR LINE, INC. *full paid and non-assessable*

transferable only on the books of this Corporation in person, or by Attorney upon surrender of this Certificate properly endorsed.

IN WITNESS WHEREOF, *the said Corporation has caused this Certificate to be signed by its duly authorized officers and its Corporate seal to be hereunto affixed this ———— day of November A.D. 1919.*

calling Garvey "without doubt, the most dangerous enemy of the Negro race in America and in the world."

Disagreements between Garvey's supporters and detractors became so intense that brawls between them broke out in Harlem. Fueling this passion was Garvey's 1922 decision to meet with Edward Young Clarke, a Ku Klux Klan leader, to solicit the Klan's support for his movement. Like the Klan, Garvey opposed racial integration, which he considered inconsistent with racial pride. However different the Klan's motives, he believed the racist group might help him fund the settlement of American blacks in Africa.

A Black Star stock certificate proclaims Africa as "the land of opportunity"—a concept that served as a magnet for black investors. As one buyer put it, he would happily "die of hunger" if by buying stock he could "better the conditions of [his] race."

In *The Philosophy and Opinions of Marcus Garvey*, Garvey expressed wry approval of the Klan. "Between the Ku Klux Klan and . . . [the whites of] the National Association for the Advancement of 'Colored' People group," he said, "give me the Klan for their honesty of purpose towards the Negro." But as a political tactic, meeting with Klan leader Clarke was disastrous, alienating many African-American leaders. In January 1923 eight influential African Americans asked the U.S. attorney general to use his "full influences completely to disband and extirpate this vicious movement [the UNIA]."

Whether this request had any direct effect is hard to say because the government had already singled out Garvey as a troublemaker. As early as 1919, Federal Bureau of Investigation director J. Edgar Hoover had suggested that the government silence Garvey by charging him with fraud in connection with the Black Star Line. In January 1922 Garvey and three other Black Star officials were indeed arrested and indicted on charges of mail fraud. Released for 15 months while the government conducted an investigation of the company, the four men were brought to trial in March 1923.

The government asserted that Garvey mailed blacks misleading advertisements for Black Star Line stock.

Black Star's flagship, the rusty old Yarmouth (*also known as the* Frederick Douglass), *enters New York harbor in 1919. "The* Yarmouth," *remarked one of her officers, "was not a vessel to set a sailor's heart aflame."*

Although he knew the company was failing, the government claimed, he continued to mail releases promising huge profits and dividends. But the government's main witness, a man who allegedly bought stock after receiving a Black Star advertisement, displayed only a vague memory of what kind of mail he had been sent.

Acting as his own lawyer, Garvey said the government had failed to prove he knowingly made false claims. He also noted that he had not profited personally from Black Star. He was convicted anyway (the other three defendants were found innocent). Garvey received the maximum sentence: a $1,000 fine and five years in prison. After serving 10 months, he was released on the order of President Calvin Coolidge, but his troubles were far from over: as soon as he walked out of jail, the government deported him. He lived in Jamaica and then moved to England, where he continued his efforts to emancipate his race.

Garvey's last years were marked by discouragement, poverty, and poor health. He died in 1940 at the age of 53, aware that his cherished projects, the Black Star Line among them, had ended in failure. But Garvey left an intellectual legacy that lived on: he elevated and expanded the race consciousness of black people around the world. He proclaimed the message of race pride and self-determination, themes that would echo in black American hearts and minds long after his departure. His writings, both in the *Negro World* and *The Philosophy and Opinions of Marcus Garvey*, inspired blacks from Harlem to Africa for generations to come.

Decades after Garvey's death, militant black leader Malcolm X had this to say: "Every time you see another nation on the African continent become independent, you know Marcus Garvey is still alive. All the freedom movements that are taking place right here in America today were initiated by the work and teachings of Marcus Garvey."

5

THAT'S ENTERTAINMENT?

While Garvey was shaking up the political scene on the East Coast, black Americans on the West Coast were slowly breaking into the film industry. Black actors were handicapped by the custom of pre–World War I Hollywood to portray black characters with white actors in blackface (makeup designed to make them look black). The use of blackface dates back to the popular 19th-century minstrel shows, which usually combined dancing, singing, and comedy. Humor in minstrel shows (also called "coon" shows) generally revolved around the exploits of a stereotypical "darky" who was always dim-witted, passive, and outsmarted by everyone around him.

An infamous example of blackface whites playing blacks is seen in director D.W. Griffith's 1915 film, *Birth of a Nation*. Based on Thomas Dixon's novel, *The Clansman*, the film is set in South Carolina during and after the Civil War. White society, its women in particular, are threatened by the hordes of blacks unleashed on the South by emancipation. The nation—and its white women—are saved by the Ku Klux Klan, whose violence is presented in the film as necessary to control the savage blacks.

The film's black characters are of two basic categories: harmless—loyal servants, amusing drunks, and fools; and dangerous—would-be rapists and killers

Two Our Gang *stars play for laughs in a typical scene from the series. Introduced in the 1920s, the wildly popular short films allowed their black and white child actors an equal chance at the heroes' roles.*

who cannot handle freedom and are easily manipu-
lated by unscrupulous northerners. White actors play
the movie's leading black roles, although actual African Americans appear in smaller parts and crowd
scenes.

Birth of a Nation so offended the NAACP that it
organized a nationwide picket campaign against it.
The organization's opposition annoyed the film's dis-
tributors but did not keep it from becoming a huge
box-office hit. More successful was the NAACP's
campaign against white actors playing black characters; from this point on, the studios' casting calls began
to include "colored" players. This was progress, but in
the eyes of many black leaders, not much; when
directors did cast black actors in black roles, those roles
were the same old stereotypes: mammies and other
faithful retainers to white families; lazy, clumsy, dull-
witted but funny "darkies"; or (much less often) vil-
lains with little on their minds but arson and rape.

Hollywood boasted no black major producer, no
black-owned studio. The first leading role in a full-
length motion picture played by a black actor was in
a 1914 film version of *Uncle Tom's Cabin*, the celebrated abolitionist novel—a best-seller in 1852, and
never out of print even today—by Harriet Beecher
Stowe. Actor Sam Lucas played the title role with an
extra dose of sentimental subservience.

"The Negro," wrote journalist Geraldyn Dismond
in a 1929 issue of *Close Up* magazine, "entered the
movies through a back door labelled 'Servants' En-
trance.'" In addition to playing contented servants,
African Americans were cast as happy, hymn-singing
field workers—often complete with standard props of
watermelon and fried chicken. Although blacks were
leaving the South in droves, films nearly always placed
them on the plantation.

One of the few exceptions to Hollywood's patron-
izing portrayal of blacks was the *Our Gang* series of

comedy shorts, which producer Hal Roach began turning out in 1922. Focusing on the adventures of a group of children, these films featured four black characters—Sunshine Sammy, Farina (named for a popular breakfast cereal), Stymie Beard, and Buckwheat. Despite their jokey names and occasionally stereotyped behavior, they were presented as equals to their white friends and were just as likely to be the heroes of any episode.

Talkies (movies with sound) revolutionized the Hollywood film industry during the 1920s, but black roles changed little. In 1929 20th Century-Fox released *Hearts of Dixie*, one of the few "black" films produced by a major studio. Describing it in his 1970 book *The Negro in Films*, critic Peter Noble asserted that *Hearts* exploited "the same old hackneyed routine, [involving] a succession of endless musical num-

Hearts of Dixie cast members demonstrate the sparkle that made this 1929 film a hit. Black actors resented the grinning, watermelon-eating characters they were usually assigned, but Hollywood's faith—and investment—in this all-black production made such stereotypes easier to bear.

bers, spirituals, prayer meetings, cotton picking and the like." The movie proved a tremendous success.

Hearts of Dixie featured comedian Stepin Fetchit (born Lincoln Theodore Monroe Andrew Perry in 1902), the first black actor to receive star billing. Fetchit's many portrayals of the old stock character—the peaceable, grinning, frequently humiliated servant—profoundly disturbed many blacks, but he vehemently defended his career. Not only had he broken down many of the barriers that kept black actors from becoming stars, he pointed out, but he had

Movie comic Stepin Fetchit (Lincoln Perry) plays a lazy worker looking for a place to nap. Strongly criticized for playing such roles, Fetchit insisted that they raised the status of blacks by making them wealthier.

become a millionaire, the first black entertainer to achieve that status.

The success of *Hearts of Dixie* was replicated by *Hallelujah*, released by Metro-Goldwyn-Mayer (MGM) the same year. The female lead, played by Nina Mae McKinney, sang her way through 40 dance sequences—all performed while picking cotton down on the farm. Making the film posed a challenge, as the script called for more than 300 singing extras and MGM boasted only one black casting director. The studio finally solved the problem by hiring the choir members from almost every black church in Los Angeles; the solution made the backlot resound with song but left the churches eerily quiet.

Not all black films came from the big Hollywood studios. A few small, white-owned, "colored" film companies made black-cast movies, designed to please audiences in the South's more than 400 black movie theaters. Successful black producers and directors were few, but their numbers included some extraordinary people. One was Oscar Micheaux. Starting out as a writer, Micheaux entered the film business after a studio showed interest in his 1917 novel, *The Homesteader*. When he failed to come to terms with the studio, Micheaux boldly decided to make the movie himself. Once started, he was hooked, making 46 films—29 silent, the rest talkies—between 1920 and 1948. (Unfortunately for film historians and fans, many of these films have been lost or destroyed.)

Micheaux was a one-man band. He wrote, directed, edited, and distributed every film he made. He shot scenes in his own apartment or in the street outside and used city parks for outdoor scenes. But raising money was always a challenge; backers usually responded more to Micheaux's considerable charisma than to any likelihood of profit. Glamorously draped in a long fur coat, he drove from one theater to the next, charming managers into showing his current film and perhaps funding his next one. Despite Micheaux's considerable business skill, his film company periodically went bankrupt, and after almost three decades of moviemaking, he called it quits in 1948. Three years later he died while on a book tour.

Another major field of entertainment that only grudgingly accepted blacks was sports. Perhaps the most famous—certainly the most infamous—black athlete of the early 1900s was boxer Jack Johnson, heavyweight champion of the world from 1908 to 1915. The first African American to hold that title (as well as the first allowed to compete for it), Johnson was a spectacular boxer who lost only 7 of his 114 professional bouts.

Johnson's incredible prowess (and his unapologetically flamboyant personality) came as something of a shock to white racists, who promptly clamored for a "great white hope" to defeat and humiliate this upstart. In 1910 Johnson fought the first of these challengers, former heavyweight champion Jim Jeffries, and beat him easily—touching off minor race riots across the country.

Johnson defied racists again by associating with white women; three of his four wives, in fact, were white. Because interracial sexual relations were taboo in the United States at this time, law authorities kept a sharp eye out for any infractions for which they could arrest the fighter. Finally, in a widely publicized series of events, one of Johnson's white wives committed

Etta Terry Duryea, first wife of World Heavyweight Champion Jack Johnson, gazes adoringly at her husband in a 1911 portrait. Johnson's many white girlfriends and wives (he had three) intensified the rage of racists who hated him simply for being black and champion at the same time.

suicide in a nightclub, and he married another white woman only three months later.

In 1912, amid great public outcry, Johnson was convicted of violating the Mann Act (which made it a federal crime to transport a woman across a state line for "immoral purposes"); he jumped bail and fled the country. He returned in 1920, served his one-year prison sentence, and went back to boxing. By that time, boxer Jack Dempsey had won the heavyweight title and had announced that he would not fight black challengers. From that point on, Johnson performed in vaudeville and at carnivals; he died in a car accident in 1946.

Despite Dempsey's example, some boxing organizations welcomed African Americans. One was the Golden Gloves, a group founded in Chicago in 1923 to help young boxers develop their talent. This organization became a springboard for many black boxers aiming for the professional ranks. Football also provided black athletes with a few opportunities: the American Professional Football Association (later the National Football League) allowed 13 black Americans to play between 1920, the year it was established, and 1930.

One prominent African-American football player was Frederick "Fritz" Pollard, a running back for Brown University who became a professional player. He was the highest paid black player in the sport, making $1,500 per game at his peak, and was later inducted into the National Football Hall of Fame. Black athletes also made a mark at the Olympics, with track star William DeHart winning a gold medal in the long jump at the 1924 games.

The basketball teams of the 20th century's first two decades were usually segregated, but black teams played white teams on an equal basis. One of the most successful was the Harlem Renaissance Five, founded in 1922. Although the "Rens" disbanded in 1948, their pioneering playing secured them a place in the Basketball Hall of Fame. Continuing to charm today's sports audiences is another independent black team established in the 1920s: the Harlem Globetrotters. Founded in 1927, the Globetrotters combine superior court skills and clowning to the delight of their many fans worldwide.

But the most popular spectator sport in post–World War I America was baseball. Although

some college teams were integrated, blacks were pointedly excluded from the major leagues. Independent black professional teams began cropping up in the 1880s, and in February 1920 Andrew "Rube" Foster, owner of Chicago's American Giants, joined with other black team owners to organize the Negro National League. Established the same year was its counterpart, the Southern Negro League. The new Negro Leagues were tremendously popular; in 1923 more than

The Harlem Globetrotters share the spotlight with owner-manager Abe Saperstein in 1930. Combining extraordinary basketball skills with slapstick comic routines, the quintet became a long-running box-office sensation.

An outstanding pitcher and brilliant promoter, Andrew "Rube" Foster is known as black baseball's founding father. In 1920 he formed the Negro National League, the nation's first professional black sports organization.

400,000 fans, mostly black, attended their games.

Black baseball was less well funded than the major leagues, but it was just as innovative. Shortstop Bill Monroe invented shin guards, shortstop William Wells invented the batting helmet, and Negro League teams held the first night games. Some of the leagues' players were nothing short of spectacular. Slugger Oscar Charleston, for example, was easily one of the decade's most powerful hitters, black or white. "When anyone asks me who was the greatest ball player, I don't have to stop to think," said former Pittsburgh Crawfords outfielder Ted Page after his retirement. "I can name him right off. His name is Oscar Charleston. . . . I'd rate Oscar Charleston over Joe DiMaggio, over Willie Mays." From 1915 to 1936, Charleston played some of the finest baseball in America.

Although Charleston was the idol of countless young blacks, black baseball's most colorful and best-known player was easily Leroy "Satchel" Paige. Paige—who hailed from Mobile, Alabama, and started with the city's Tigers in 1924—was a tremendous pitcher who talked as fast as he threw. "If I had been pitching to [batters Babe] Ruth and [Lou] Gehrig," he once remarked, "you could knock a few points off those big lifetime batting averages." Other players agreed. One recalled that Paige's "arms were so long, he'd raise up that big foot and the next thing you'd know the ball was by ya."

Paige was not only quick; he endured. His career spanned decades, and when the major leagues finally admitted black players in 1947, Paige—by this time in his 40s—was among the first to be signed up.

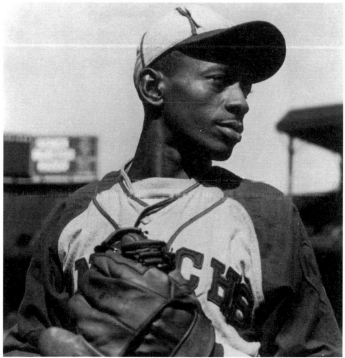

Legendary pitcher and perennial crowd-pleaser Leroy "Satchel" Paige was also a humorist and philosopher. Among his memorable pronouncements was the much-quoted advice, "And don't look back. Something might be gaining on you."

According to Robert Peterson's *Only the Ball Was White* (1970), fans and other players often asked Paige how he managed to stay so youthful. His reply was recorded by a sportswriter:

> Avoid fried meats, which angry up the blood.
> If your stomach disputes you, lie down and pacify it with cool thoughts.
> Keep the juices flowing by jangling gently as you move.
> Go very light on the vices, such as carrying on in society— the society ramble ain't restful.
> Avoid running at all times.
> And don't look back. Something might be gaining on you.

Blacks played baseball all over the country, but from 1900 to the end of the 1920s, they began to focus their attention on the Northeast. Word spread of a glamorous black neighborhood in New York City sometimes called "the Negro capital of the world." It was better known as Harlem.

6

HARLEM

W hat a crowd! All classes and colors met face to face, ultra aristocrats, Bourgeois, Communists, Park Avenuers galore, bookers, publishers, Broadway celebs, and Harlemites giving each other the once over. The social revolution was on." So wrote Geraldyn Dismond in the *Interstate Tattler*, capturing in a few words the lively potpourri of Harlem in its heyday. Dismond was describing a party at entertainer Taylor Gordon's, but it could easily have been one of the many gatherings held at the home of heiress A'Lelia Walker or novelist Jessie Fauset or white writer and critic Carl Van Vetchen. After World War I, the African-American political revolution had made news, but by 1925, culture was the talk of the town.

> **The names tell the story. Langston Hughes, Zora Neale Hurston, Claude McKay, Ethel Waters, Countee Cullen, Bessie Smith, Jean Toomer, Duke Ellington, Louis Armstrong, and many, many other black writers, singers, poets,**

Cast members of the Smalls's Paradise Club floorshow acknowledge audience applause in 1929. Unlike many of the era's Harlem night spots, Smalls's—where orders were delivered by roller-skating waiters—catered to black and white patrons in equal numbers.

Millionaire heiress A'Lelia Walker shows off one of her high-style outfits in the late 1920s. Sometimes called the "Great Black Empress," Walker hosted the flashiest parties in town.

painters, and musicians settled in Harlem during the 1920s and created one of the greatest cultural outpourings in American history. The Harlem social scene, the glamour of its nightlife, and, most important, the art it produced were all part of a period that came to be known as the Harlem Renaissance. African-American artistic identity asserted itself early in the 1920s, reached its peak in 1928, and—along with much of American culture—crashed to a halt in the Great Depression of the 1930s.

The neighborhood of Harlem is located in the northern part of Manhattan, New York City's central borough. In the 1920s Harlem centered on 135th Street and 7th Avenue and reached from 110th Street to 150th Street. The area stretched from the East River to St. Nicholas Avenue on the west, a space of less than two square miles.

The Harlem Renaissance was in many ways the result of the Great Migration. Thanks to migrants from the South, New York's black neighborhoods were getting more and more crowded. At the same time, in the middle-class white district known as Harlem, real estate speculators were bidding up property prices far beyond their actual value. The bubble burst around 1910. As prices plummeted, Harlem building owners panicked.

Entering the volatile Harlem scene at this point were a number of black realtors. Among them was Philip A. Payton, Jr., who, along with other fast-moving entrepreneurs, knew he could make large profits by opening this desirable neighborhood to blacks. Payton established the Afro-American Realty Company, leased or bought several Harlem buildings, and began renting to blacks. His move accelerated the local real estate panic; the remaining white property owners, sure that the presence of blacks would permanently depress prices, sold for what they could get and fled.

Of course, so many sellers brought still lower property prices, and black realtors began snapping up even more bargains. (Ironically, those white landlords who stayed in Harlem began renting to blacks and made out very well. At this point, Harlem was far and away the choicest area for settlement open to blacks. Because prejudice and custom sharply limited the neighborhoods available to them, the attractive places brought rents proportionately higher than those paid by whites, who had many more choices.)

But Harlem's whites did not surrender the neighborhood without a fight. The president of the Harlem Property Owners Protective Association led the attack, discouraging Harlem property owners from selling or renting to African Americans and even offering to build a 24-foot-high fence at 136th Street to keep blacks out of the neighborhood. A local newspaper, the *Harlem Home News,* shrilly announced in July 1911 that white homeowners "must wake up and get busy before it is too late to repel the black hordes that stand ready to destroy the homes and scatter the fortunes of the whites living and doing business in the very heart of Harlem." But by that time Harlem was already the neighborhood of choice for New York's African Americans.

St. Philips, New York's major black church, followed its parishioners to Harlem, buying up choice pieces of property. Black newspapers soon moved their offices to Harlem, too, as did African-American social clubs and political organizations. Thus was born *the* Harlem, a city within a city.

Despite the glamorous image of the Harlem Renaissance, the typical Harlemite never received an invitation to A'Lelia Walker's home. Many Harlem residents were black southerners and Afro-Caribbean people who came to New York to escape poverty. But even to poorer residents, Harlem was like a promised land. Migrants sent home letters singing the community's praises. They visited their old homes wearing stylish clothes and telling stories about the good life in Harlem, where black people owned businesses and the streets were patrolled by police who shared their culture and color. In Harlem black people could be themselves, outside the constant scrutiny of white America, and acting humble in order to placate racist whites was not necessary.

An anonymous poet captured Harlem's liberating qualities in a song of praise to the two-square-mile area:

Chant another song of Harlem;
Not about the wrong of Harlem
But about the throng of Harlem,
Proud that they belong to Harlem;
They, the over-blamed of Harlem
Need not be ashamed of Harlem;
All is not ill-famed in Harlem,
The devil, too, is tamed in Harlem.

A Harlem policeman directs traffic in 1925. The presence of black officials helped make Harlem a magnet for thousands of African Americans during the "Roaring Twenties."

Of course, most ordinary Harlem residents did not strike it rich in this promised land. Beneath the glittering façade was the tough life of working people, the domestics, barbers, numbers runners, laborers, and other less affluent men and women. Rents were high. A Harlem apartment cost $12 to $30 more a month than similar housing in other parts of Manhattan, and simply paying the rent could cost a typical working-class family 40 percent of its income. Many families took in borders, and housing was nearly always over-crowded.

One innovative approach to making ends meet was the rent party, an event held in a private home for which admission—anywhere from a dime to 50 cents—was charged. If the party was successful, the rent could be paid for another month. On weekends several rent parties on the same block often competed for customers, and a host's reputation for providing good liquor or good music could make or break the party. Entertainment was often amateur and organized at a moment's notice. As cabbage and ham hocks were served to all comers, jazz bands played and singers got their chance for momentary recognition.

Harlem residents get together for a block party about 1915. Such festivities, along with the always popular "rent parties"— given to help tenants hold onto their apartments—were a regular feature of Harlem life during the years between the world wars.

Rent-party hosts advertised by handing out flyers in Harlem. One such invitation read:

Papa is mad about the way you do,
So meet the gang and Skoodle um Skoo.
If you can't Charleston or do the pigeon wing
You sure can shake that thing.
If you can't hold your Man,
Don't cry after he's gone,
Just find another.
You don't get nothing for being an angel child,
So you might as well get real busy and real wild.

Rent parties featured not only the popular Charleston and pigeon-wing dances but the more intimate "slow dragging" dancing all through the night. Besides providing a good time for customers, rent parties developed a sense of camaraderie and fellowship in what could otherwise be an impersonal urban area. After all, the person who paid admission to a rent party might be asking others to pay for entry at her home the following week. Through these lively gatherings, connections were made, romances begun, and community well-being fostered. As the writer Wallace Thurman pointed out, the rent party was "as essential to 'low' Harlem as the cultural receptions and soirees . . . [were] to 'high' Harlem."

As Thurman's comment implies, black Harlem was never classless; status divided Harlemites as surely as it did downtowners. But even those who were struggling to keep their heads above water saw Harlem as a place of opportunity. Harlem's nicknames—the city of refuge, the Negro Mecca, Black Manhattan—reflected a pride of place; a Harlemite might be poor, but at least he was poor in Harlem. This optimism, combined with Harlem's vibrant nightlife and poli-

tics, captured the imagination of writers and intellectuals around the world. The area's cabarets, churches,
political clubs, and street corners inspired innumer-
able writers, painters, and musicians.

The Harlem cabarets, for example, were centers of
lively, high-quality performances that sometimes attracted more attention from downtown white patrons
than from the locals. Ed Smalls's Paradise Club, the
most prestigious black-owned nightspot, provided
dancing waiters, and the most famous of the cabarets,
the Cotton Club, drew larger crowds than the shows
on Broadway. It was also a Jim Crow establishment;
black dancers, musicians, comedians, and other artists
performed for an exclusively white audience and were
paid by the club's white owner, gangster Owney Mad-
den. Jimmy Durante, a well-known comedian, expressed the familiar prejudice of the time when he
defended the exclusion of black patrons, claiming
"nobody wants razors, blackjacks, or fists flying—and
the chances of a war are less if there's no mixing."

The Cotton Club's Jim Crow policy reflected a
certain truth about Harlem's famed nightlife, namely
that whites often viewed the area as a place to escape
the constraints of public opinion and "respectability"
that might govern their behavior in a predominantly
white area. One explanation for this view is that the
clubs and cabarets of Harlem almost always served
alcohol, which was illegal after 1919, when the nation
ratified the 18th, or Prohibition, Amendment to the
Constitution.

White attendance was also encouraged by Harlem's reputation—encouraged by club owners and
managers—for being a place without rules. Clubs
booked exotic and ribald dancers, comedians, and
singers, among them the notorious Gladys Bently, a
female chanteuse who impersonated a man. In order
to get bookings, performers often made their acts even
racier. A singer might rewrite lyrics to make them

Headliner Earl "Snakehips" Tucker struts his stuff in a Harlem club during the late 1920s. When Tucker danced, he gyrated his pelvis so fast that the whirling tassel on his belt became a blur.

more suggestive, for example, or band members might perform off-color skits between sets.

Harlem's wild reputation worked to the advantage of some of its residents (gay and lesbian Harlemites attained a level of visibility unheard of elsewhere during the 1920s), but not everybody was pleased. W. E. B. Du Bois, for example, publicly disdained Harlem's rakish nightlife, which he felt fed the racist stereotype that all blacks were immoral and oversexed. Like many other staid Harlemites, Du Bois shunned the nightclubs, preferring to brighten his weekends with a Sunday stroll up Harlem's main street, Seventh Avenue.

Du Bois did not walk alone on Seventh Avenue between 125th and 138th streets. Strollers could easily meet nearly everyone they knew on a Sunday afternoon, and everybody was dressed to impress. "Sunday best"—furs, feathers, bright shawls, and three-piece suits cut to perfection—was the norm. Like Du Bois, some of the promenaders were relatively well-off, but many were not. Those with limited incomes took advantage of installment plans offered at local stores, which allowed waitresses, carpenters, and the lowest-paid laborers to equal their economic betters in what novelist Rudolph Fisher called "procession wild" Harlem. "Indeed," observed Fisher, "even Fifth Avenue on Easter never quite attains this; practice makes perfect, and Harlem's Seventh Avenue boasts fifty-two Easters a year."

This was the Harlem that attracted black writers, artists, intellectuals, and other ambitious men and women from across the country and the seas. Like every city, Harlem also attracted its share of con men, drug dealers, and charlatans of every make. But Harlem in the 1920s was a special place, a place where African-American men and women could see each other in their full humanity. Harlemites felt that the area belonged to them.

When West Indian scholar and political activist Hubert Harrison stood on the corner of 135th Street and Lenox Avenue and preached pan-Africanism, he spoke to a receptive audience in a protected space. Such encounters occurred all over Harlem. Within

this environment, self-reflective thought could take place, and individuals could escape the ever-present racism found beyond the boundaries. Bookshops sprang up to meet black peoples' needs; black churches filled their souls with spirituals and prayers; black journalists wrote for black-run newspapers; educational forums drew enormous crowds.

This was the social setting, the hothouse atmosphere in which the Harlem Renaissance grew. The novelists, poets, musicians, and other artists who flocked to Harlem during the 1920s made it synonymous with the creative spirit, but they could not have survived without this inspiration from its gritty, colorful, noisy streets. For African Americans in the 1920s, Harlem symbolized freedom in all its forms.

Customers crowd the bar at Harlem's popular Big Apple Restaurant. Newcomers, many of them from the intolerant South, found the free-and-easy atmosphere of African America's "capital" almost too good to believe.

7

RENAISSANCE

In 1920s Harlem, poets, singers, novelists, sculptors, painters, and musicians working on every corner, in small rooms on every block, were creating the Harlem Renaissance. Black artists, who absorbed Harlem's race pride and interest in African and African-American traditions, interacted with intellectuals, other artists, and ordinary Harlemites. The result was an explosion of artistic expression.

Although the Harlem Renaissance involved a blossoming of all the arts, it is perhaps best known as a literary movement. Young novelists and poets were supported and promoted by older established figures (many of whom were writers themselves) including Du Bois, White, Randolph, James Weldon Johnson, Charles S. Johnson, and Alain Locke. Du Bois's *Crisis*, Charles Johnson's *Opportunity* (the journal of the National Urban League), and Randolph's *Messenger* published many new, young writers, and broadly connected people such as White persuaded mainstream publishers to print stories, essays, and poetry by black writers.

Indeed, one of the seminal events of the Harlem Renaissance was the 1925 publication of *Survey Graphic*, a special edition dedicated solely to celebrat-

Pictured at the height of the Renaissance, this street scene suggests the excitement, grit, and glamour that attracted African Americans to Harlem.

ing the new generation of black writers. Alain Locke, a Howard University professor and the first African-American Rhodes Scholar, edited the magazine, whose contents were published later that year as the book *The New Negro*. In his introduction to the book, Locke said he considered the new writers' work important to the political progress of African Americans:

> The especially cultural recognition [that these writers] win should in turn prove the key to that revaluation of the Negro which must precede or accompany any considerable further betterment of race relationships. But whatever the general effect, the present generation will have added the motives of self-expression and spiritual development to the old and still unfinished task of making material headway and progress.

Although the two generations worked together, the older often publicly feuded with the younger over what subjects they should handle. The senior writers (notably Du Bois) felt that black authors should strive to present black characters in a positive light, avoiding stories about criminals or rogues—especially if whites were likely to read the work. But younger writers, such as poets and novelists Claude McKay and Langston Hughes, felt that this deliberately sunny view was artistically dishonest. Hughes, writing for *The Nation* magazine in a 1926 article entitled "The Negro Artist and the Racial Mountain," declared:

> We younger Negro artists who create now intend to express our individual dark-skinned selves without fear or shame. If white people are pleased, we are glad. If they are not, it doesn't matter. We know we are beautiful. And ugly too. If colored people are pleased, we are glad. If they are not, their displeasure doesn't matter either.

Yet the displeasure of blacks could be quite forceful. Hughes himself noted, in his 1940 autobiography, *The Big Sea*, that his 1927 poetry collection, *Fine Clothes to the Jew*, which dealt with the seedy side of Harlem life, prompted headlines in the black press that read LANGSTON HUGHES' BOOK OF POEMS TRASH and LANGSTON HUGHES—THE SEWER DWELLER. And Du Bois, in a *Crisis* review of McKay's 1928 novel, *Home to Harlem*, reported that the novel "for the most part nauseates me, and after the dirtier parts of its filth I feel distinctly like taking a bath."

But McKay was not the sort of writer who feared controversy. Born in the hills of Jamaica in 1890, McKay was the youngest of 11 children. His parents indulged his early interests in poetry, and by age 10 he was writing verse and performing for elementary-school crowds. In 1912, after winning local attention as a poet, McKay made his way to the United States to study agriculture at Alabama's Tuskegee Institute. But he was soon seized by what he described in his 1937 autobiography, *A Long Way from Home,* as "the lust to wander and wonder . . . to achieve something new, something in the spirit and accent of America."

Claude McKay headed for Harlem in 1914. "Harlem was my first positive reaction to American life," he wrote in a 1928 article for *McClure's* magazine. "It was like entering a paradise of my own people." He worked as a bartender, longshoreman, and dining car waiter on the Pennsylvania Railroad, writing poems whenever he found spare moments.

Philosopher, college professor, and author Alain Leroy Locke, a central figure of the Harlem Renaissance, wrote many articles and several books. Probably best known were The New Negro *(1925) and* The Negro in American Culture *(published in 1956, two years after Locke's death).*

Becoming committed to socialism, McKay published some poetry in the left-wing journal the *Liberator*. The most famous of these was his 1919 poem "If We Must Die," a militant call for self-defense against

American racist violence. (The poem received re-
newed acclaim during World War II, when Prime
Minister Winston Churchill of Britain quoted it to
help rally his countrymen against the threat of a
German invasion.) "If We Must Die," which made
McKay an instant literary celebrity, reads in part:

> If we must die—let it not be like hogs
> Hunted and penned in an inglorious spot. . . .
> Like men we'll face the murderous cowardly pack,
> Pressed to the wall, dying, but fighting back!

Many critics consider McKay's 1922 poetry collection, *Harlem Shadows*, the first major literary work of
the Harlem Renaissance. Reviewing the volume in
the *New York Age*, James Weldon Johnson said, "No
Negro poet has sung more beautifully of his race than
McKay and no poet has ever equalled the power with
which he expresses the bitterness that so often rises in
the heart of the race."

But for the ever-restless McKay, not even his
Harlem "paradise" provided enough satisfaction. He
left New York in 1922 for the Soviet Union to witness
communism firsthand, and then moved to France,
living first in Paris and then Marseilles. Although he
was overseas during most of the Harlem Renaissance,
he continued to write about Harlem, later claiming
in *A Long Way from Home*, "I had done my best Harlem
stuff when I was abroad, seeing it from a long per-
spective."

While McKay was living in France, he published
Home to Harlem, an examination of Harlem's under-
world that, despite Du Bois's disapprobation, became
a best-seller and was at the time the most popular
novel ever written by a black artist. McKay published
three more books—*Banjo* (1929), a novel about poor
blacks in Marseilles; *Gingertown* (1932), a collection

Author and teacher Jessie Fauset, sometimes called the "midwife of the Harlem Renaissance" (left), poet Langston Hughes (center), and novelist/anthropologist Zora Neale Hurston meet near a statue of educator Booker T. Washington at Alabama's Tuskegee Institute in 1927.

of short stories, half of which are set in Harlem; and *Banana Bottom* (1933), a novel set in Jamaica—before returning to the United States in 1934.

McKay's work continued to generate controversy among black critics: the *New York Amsterdam News*, which was one of the few black papers to positively review *Home to Harlem*, dismissed *Banjo* as "Coon stuff." But McKay was unperturbed, stating in a 1928 letter to James Weldon Johnson, "We must leave the appreciation of what we are doing to the emancipated Negro intelligentsia of the future."

McKay's view was undoubtedly shared by Langston Hughes. Born in Joplin, Missouri, in 1902, Hughes never had a stable family life. He found an early solace in literature; according to *The Big Sea*, he began to "believe in nothing but books, and the wonderful world in books—where if people suffered, they suffered in beautiful language, not the monosyllables, as we did in Kansas." He spent his high school years in Cleveland, where his books, poetry, and charming personality got him through.

Harlem-born poet Countee Porter Cullen, another Renaissance star, published his first poem at 15; by the time he graduated from college his work had appeared in the nation's top magazines and bagged a score of literary prizes. Cullen's popularity continued until his death in 1946 at the age of 43.

Hughes's words attracted Harlem's notice long before he arrived there himself. Aboard a train to Mexico in 1920, Hughes crossed the Mississippi River and began writing a poem that would become his celebrated "The Negro Speaks of Rivers." The 19-year-old poet sent his work to Jessie Redmon Fauset, a prolific and well-respected novelist then serving as the *Crisis* literary editor. In the magazine's March 1926 issue, Fauset write that she "took [Hughes's] beautiful dignified creation to Dr. Du Bois" and asked him, "What colored person is there . . . in the United States who writes like that and yet is unknown to us?"

The next year Hughes arrived in New York, purportedly to study mining at Columbia University but, according to *The Big Sea*, "mainly because [he] wanted to see Harlem." Promptly ushered into the literary scene, he was introduced to numerous critics and writers. Not surprisingly, he spent more time attending plays, concerts, lectures, and literary debates than studying, and he left Columbia in 1922.

Hughes's writing career was launched in 1925, when his poem "The Weary Blues" won a literary contest sponsored by *Opportunity* magazine. A year later, he published his first poetry collection, *The Weary Blues*, followed the next year by *Fine Clothes to the Jew*. Hughes continued to work, producing numerous novels, plays, children's books, autobiographical works, and poetry collections in the years up to his death in 1967.

Hughes's poetry was revolutionary in its use of jazz and blues rhythms and idioms as well as the cadences of Harlem street talk. Such material distressed some black critics, but Hughes felt that African-American folk culture needed to be celebrated. His appreciation of black culture was pointed out by his friend Arna Bontemps, the poet and critic who, in a 1952 *Saturday Review* article, claimed that "Few people have enjoyed being Negro as much as Langston Hughes. . . . He would not have missed the experience of being what he is for the world."

Hughes's interest in folk culture was enthusiastically shared by one of the most lively personalities of the Harlem Renaissance, Zora Neale Hurston. Hurston wrote her best-known works—her novels, especially *Their Eyes Were Watching God*—in the 1930s and 1940s, but during the 1920s she wrote short stories, collaborated on plays, and helped found the avant-garde literary magazine *Fire!!* Her personality and intelligence were by all accounts captivating. Hughes claimed in *The Big Sea*:

> Only to reach a wider audience, need she ever write books—because she is a perfect book of entertainment in herself. In her youth she was always getting scholarships and things from wealthy white people, some of whom simply paid her just to sit around and represent the Negro race for them, she did it in such a racy fashion.

Born in Eatonville, Florida, Hurston came to Harlem in 1924 from Howard University, where Alain Locke had encouraged her to go to New York. She arrived with a satchel full of manuscripts, but she soon became an active folklorist and anthropologist, and she would ultimately combine the two disciplines by effectively using southern folklore and language in her novels. During the late 1920s she studied at Barnard College with the famous anthropologist Franz Boas, and she became locally famous for her attempt to disprove a theory that black people had smaller brains:

standing on a Harlem street corner, she measured the head of anyone willing to lend theirs for a quick sizing up.

But the best-known Harlem writer of the 1920s was easily Countee Cullen. Graceful, brilliant, and gregarious, Cullen was also a far more traditional poet than Hughes or McKay. He wrote in conventional rhymed stanzas, and the Harlem establishment much preferred his subject matter—often African-American spirituality—to McKay's radicalism or Hughes's street scenes. Cullen is a somewhat mysterious figure to biographers, as he lied freely about his background, and definitive records of his childhood have never been found.

Cullen was probably born in Louisville, Kentucky, in 1903. Orphaned at an early age, he moved as a teenager to Harlem, where Carolyn Cullen and her husband, the Reverend Frederick Cullen, adopted him. Countee's adoptive father was pastor of Harlem's Salem Methodist Episcopal Church, which had some 2,500 members by the mid-1920s. A well-respected member of the community, Frederick Cullen was also a long-standing member of the NAACP.

Although his father's connections no doubt helped his career, Cullen proved prodigiously talented, winning nearly every poetry prize available to students. By the time he graduated from New York University in 1925, he was being published regularly. His first collection, *Color*, appeared to great critical acclaim in 1925. Cullen received a master of arts degree from Harvard University and began working as an assistant editor for *Opportunity* the next year. In 1927, he published two poetry collections, *Copper Sun* and *The Ballad of the Brown Girl*, as well as editing an anthology of black poetry, *Carolling Dusk*. His last poetry collection, *The Black Christ and Other Poems*, was published in 1929. Cullen's output of poetry ended with the Harlem Renaissance, but he later wrote children's books and a novel.

Louis "Satchmo" Armstrong displays his trademarks—a trumpet and a dazzling smile—in 1929. In a career spanning more than half the 20th century (he died in 1971), Armstrong achieved a "crossover" popularity matched by few musicians of any era.

McKay, Hughes, Hurston, and Cullen were only a few of the renaissance's outstanding writers of prose and poetry. Among others were novelists Nella Larsen, Wallace Thurman, and Rudolph Fisher and poets Jean Toomer and Georgia Douglas Johnson. Larsen, the first black woman to receive a Guggenheim Fellowship, used her novels *Quicksand* (1928) and *Passing* (1929) to focus on the dilemmas of light-skinned, middle-class African Americans. Novelist and editor Thurman dissected Harlem society's color discrimination in *The Blacker the Berry* (1929); poet and novelist Toomer wrote the experimental *Cane* (1923); feminist poet Johnson's works include *The Heart of a Woman* (1918) and *Bronze* (1922); Fisher, a medical doctor, made use of his technical knowledge in his second novel, the first all-black detective story, *The Conjure-Man Dies: A Mystery Tale of Dark Harlem* (1932).

Surrounding these writers was a powerful resurgence of black theater. *Shuffle Along*, a musical comedy written by Eubie Blake and Noble Sissle, opened to great success on Broadway in 1921. Its success led to Broadway productions of a number of other black-themed shows (often written by blacks but produced and directed by whites), including *Plantation Review*, *Chocolate Kiddies* (with music by band leader Duke Ellington), *Dover Street to Dixie*, *From Dixie to Broadway*, and *Blackbirds*.

Written primarily for white audiences, many of these productions have been criticized for their stereotyped characters and minstrel-like musical numbers. Nonetheless, the shows established a number of black singers and dancers (most famously Florence Mills) as bona fide stars. Serious nonmusical theater also thrived. A number of smaller theater groups performed in Harlem, providing national fame for such actors as Charles Gilpin and Paul Robeson, who appeared in Eugene O'Neill's *The Emperor Jones*.

Musicals formed only part of the increasingly important black music scene. One of the era's most celebrated musical forms was jazz, the New Orleans-born sound so widely heard that novelist F. Scott Fitzgerald dubbed the 1920s "The Jazz Age." When jazz began developing in the 1890s and early 1900s, New Orleans was notable both for its diverse ethnic mix and its musical character. At the turn of the century, with a population of only 200,000 people, the city had 30 full-sized orchestras and countless smaller bands and groups.

At some point in the early 20th century, local black musicians began to give popular music a new twist. They continued to use the horns and percussion instruments of marching bands, but now they began to "swing" the tunes—to use different times for different instruments in the band, creating a complex interplay of rhythms. The new music, known as jazz or Dixieland, was loud, brassy, and popular. It was most commonly heard in Storyville, a seedy New Orleans district where musicians polished their art and brothel-keepers used it to lure customers.

One such musician was Louis Armstrong, who was born in New Orleans around 1900. When he was still a baby, his father deserted Armstrong and his teen-aged mother. Raised largely in Storyville, where his mother worked, Armstrong was poor in material things but rich in music. For a while, he and his mother lived on the same block as Union Son's Hall—better known as Funky Butt Hall—one of the city's well-known dance clubs.

Blues "empress" Bessie Smith gives a characteristically high-powered performance around 1924. "That wasn't a voice she had," recalled one jazz critic, "it was a flamethrower licking out across the room."

When Armstrong was a teenager, he was arrested for firing a pistol in the street. Sentenced to two years in the Colored Waifs' Home, a reform school run by black social workers, he joined the institution's brass band and learned to play the cornet and other instruments. After his discharge, Armstrong worked at a variety of menial jobs during the day and played cornet at night, first in "tonks" (where the music was sometimes interrupted by gunfights), then in street bands, and finally in the city's better jazz bands.

Armstrong's extraordinary musical skill made other musicians sit up and take notice. Among his admirers were such prominent locals as trombonist and band leader Edward "Kid" Ory, pianist Jelly Roll Morton, cornetist Freddie Keppard, clarinetist Sidney Bechet, and, most important, cornetist and band leader Joe "King" Oliver. But by the time World War I ended in late 1918, many of these musicians had left New Orleans. Concerned about the health and safety of the thousands of sailors stationed in the city, the War Department had forced the closing of the New Orleans brothels, thereby sharply limiting opportunities for musicians. Many sought work in other cities.

Armstrong remained in his hometown until 1922, when he received an invitation from Oliver, who had gone to Chicago in 1918, to join his Creole Jazz Band. Jazz had flourished in Chicago, and the city's South Side was home to numerous former New Orleans stars. As the mostly self-taught New Orleans musicians taught Dixieland jazz to their more classically trained Chicago counterparts, the music's sound became more polished and sophisticated—resulting in "Chicago-style" jazz.

In addition, the blues—originally a black folk music that used a special musical scale with certain "bent" or flattened notes—was also in ascendance. Such singers as Ma Rainey (known as the Mother of the Blues), Bessie Smith (Empress of the Blues), Trixie

Edward Kennedy "Duke" Ellington (at piano) and his orchestra take a break at Harlem's Cotton Club in 1930. Perhaps more than any other musician, Ellington helped make jazz a popular American art form.

Smith, Clara Smith (the three Smiths were not related), Ethel Waters, and Alberta Hunter toured the country and made popular records (Bessie Smith alone sold nearly 10 million records). Jazz musicians nearly always accompanied the blues singers of the 1920s, and the two types of music readily commingled.

Armstrong and the Creole Jazz Band were at the center of this burgeoning music scene, playing at Chicago's Lincoln Gardens, a black dance hall. Although the band's members were talented musicians, they had little formal training. Lil Hardin (who became the second of Armstrong's four wives) recalled that when she joined the band as a pianist she asked for written music. "They politely told me they didn't have any," Hardin remembered. "I then asked what key would the first number be in. I must have been speaking another language because [Oliver] said, 'When you hear two knocks, just start to play.'"

After two years in Chicago, Armstrong went to New York to play with the Fletcher Henderson Orchestra, a considerably larger band that played in the city's prestigious Roseland Ballroom. Armstrong stayed with Henderson's band for a year, then moved back to Chicago in 1925 and with a small group of musicians made a number of records that changed the face of jazz. The records featured a good deal of solo playing, rather than the ensemble work that was more common at the time. In his solos, Armstrong readily demonstrated his genius for improvisation, which although relatively common due to the musical illiteracy of many jazz musicians, had never before been considered as desirable in—much less essential to—jazz. Armstrong's pioneering performance on the 1925 records changed the way musicians played and perceived jazz music.

More musical history started in 1927, when New York's Cotton Club decided to compete with Roseland for jazz fans—and signed a new house band, Duke Ellington and His Orchestra. Edward Kennedy "Duke" Ellington, the band's suave, handsome leader and pianist, hailed from Washington, D.C., where he had enjoyed a comfortable upbringing in a doting family. As a youth, Ellington had no particular interest in playing music, preferring baseball and art. But one summer the teenager heard jazz pianist Harvey Brooks perform and promptly decided to become a musician.

Ellington had had some formal piano training as a child, so he returned to the instrument, teaching himself how to "swing" and composing his own tunes. Becoming enamored of stride piano, a style of playing that fell somewhere between jazz and the earlier ragtime music, Ellington befriended many well-known stride pianists, including James P. Johnson, Fats Waller, and Willie "the Lion" Smith. By the time he graduated from high school in 1918, Ellington was not only playing professionally but had become a successful agent who booked performances for other musicians. In 1923 Ellington and some fellow Washington musicians moved to Harlem, where they landed a job at Barron's Exclusive Club. From there, the men moved downtown to the Kentucky Club, and then returned to Harlem to play the Cotton Club.

Ellington's band played a key role in popularizing jazz, regularly making live radio broadcasts of their performances that were heard all over the East Coast. The ensemble specialized in so-called jungle-style jazz, which featured musician James "Bubber" Miley's growling trumpet (the growl was produced by covering and uncovering the bell of the horn with a common plunger). Ellington himself proved both a talented arranger and a prolific songwriter. His "East St. Louis Toodle-oo" and "Black and Tan Fantasy" (both cowritten with Miley) are only two of his many jazz tunes from the 1920s that are now considered classics. Despite their tremendous successes in the 1920s, both Ellington and Armstrong were only beginning their musical careers, both of which would span the decades until their deaths in the 1970s.

Ultimately, the Harlem Renaissance cannot be understood through a simple description of individual artists and what they produced. In Harlem, the 1920s moved with the spirit, the hard work, the joys, and the sorrows of thousands of black Americans living in a society that largely rejected their contributions. To be sure, white patrons, publishers, and intellectuals encouraged and promoted black artists. But the Harlem Renaissance was a profoundly black and profoundly shared experience. Political assertiveness, race pride, and a growing respect for African culture fueled the renaissance. The famous and the anonymous alike contributed to this flowering of African-American culture—a collective achievement equaled nowhere else during the 20th century.

8

A NEW STRUGGLE BEGINS

In the introduction of his 1922 anthology, *The Book of American Negro Poetry*, James Weldon Johnson made some challenging assertions about race and creativity:

> No people that has produced great literature and art has ever been looked upon by the world as distinctly inferior. ... The status of the Negro in the United States is more a question of national mental attitude toward the race than of actual conditions. And nothing will do more to change that mental attitude and raise his status than a demonstration of intellectual parity [equality] by the Negro through the production of literature and art.

Langston Hughes, writing with the benefit of hindsight in *The Big Sea* (1948), mocked Johnson's contentions:

> Some Harlemites thought the millennium had come. ... They thought the race problem had at last been solved through Art plus Gladys Bently. They were sure the New Negro would lead a new life from then on in green pastures of tolerance created by Countee Cullen, Ethel Waters, Claude McKay, Duke Ellington, [Broadway star Bill] Bojangles, and Alain Locke.

Exuberant youngsters congregate outside their Harlem school in 1925. Despite its modest economic position, the community's overall mood in this era was optimistic; "Everyone was having a grand time," wrote novelist Wallace Thurman. "The second emancipation seemed inevitable."

Author, editor, and NAACP chief James Weldon Johnson firmly believed that African Americans could rise only through the arts. "The final measure of the greatness of all peoples," he said, "is the amount and standard of the literature and art they have produced."

Hughes's bitterness stemmed from the Great Depression of the 1930s, which wiped out thousands of businesses and banks and reduced millions of Americans to poverty. Hardest hit, not surprisingly, by the economic devastation was the African-American community. Many blacks had held service-sector jobs—as street sweepers, cleaners, servants, elevator operators—which were always the first jobs eliminated in hard times. Early layoffs also included the blacks who had recently broken into the industrial world.

According to a 1930 *New York Herald Tribune* report, the 1929 stock market crash—the immediate cause of the depression—had "produced five times as much unemployment in Harlem as in other parts of the city." By the end of 1930, 50 percent of the African-American population was out of work in Harlem and in Cleveland, Ohio; the figure rose to 60 percent in Detroit and St. Louis. And unemployment was not the only burden to fall disproportionately on the black community. During the 1930s, African Americans experienced higher rates of illness, infant death, malnutrition, and suicide than whites. Even more ominously, lynchings increased as whites attacked blacks whom they regarded as competitors for employment.

Even black people who were desperately poor to begin with were hurt by the depression. In her autobiographical *I Know Why the Caged Bird Sings* (1970), author Maya Angelou recalled the depression's effects on her hometown of Stamps, Arkansas, where most of the blacks were farmers.

> The Depression must have hit the white section of Stamps with a cyclonic impact, but it seeped into the black area slowly, like a thief with misgivings. The country had been in the throes of the Depression for two years before the Negroes in Stamps knew it. I think that everyone thought that the Depression, like everything else, was for the whitefolks, so it had nothing to do with them. Our people had lived off the land and counted on cotton-picking and hoeing and chopping seasons to bring in the cash needed to buy shoes, clothes, books and light farm equipment. It was when the owners of cotton fields dropped the payment of ten cents for a pound of cotton to eight, seven and finally five that the Negro community realized that the Depression, at least, did not discriminate.

Because they were thrown off land they had worked but did not own, southern tenant farmers felt the depression's effects quickly. In 1930 a drought hit the South, worsening an already grim economic situation. Many rural southern blacks migrated to the cities, where they competed for increasingly scarce jobs.

Black churches and institutions such as the National Urban League did their best to ease the suffering. In several cities, the league established job-training programs and community centers for the needy. League workers found families housing, distributed clothes, fought evictions, provided loans, and set up programs for better playgrounds and public health.

Black churches were even more critical for keeping life and limb in order and hope alive. In Harlem, the United Holy Church of America offered food and clothing to needy families, no questions asked. Harlem's largest black church, the 8,000-member-strong Abyssinian Baptist church, also contributed heavily to ease the suffering. The church was headed by the Reverend Adam Clayton Powell, Sr., a charismatic and committed clergyman who grew up in the South, took over midtown New York's Abyssinian Baptist Church in 1908, and moved it to Harlem in 1922.

Powell's influence and ability to help his people was felt everywhere in the community. He worked hard to build a home for the elderly, raised money for black schools and hospitals, and offered an appealing message of hard work, education, and concern for those who were less well off. As soon as the depression hit, Powell demanded that black churches, including his own, do more for the needy. "The ax is laid at the root of the tree," he thundered, "and this unemployed mass of black men, led by a hungry God, will

In her autobiography, I Know Why the Caged Bird Sings, *dancer, songwriter, and author Maya Angelou commented wryly on the black community's economic hardships in the 1930s: "The Depression, at least, did not discriminate."*

come to the Negro churches looking for fruit and finding none, will say cut it down and cast it into the fire."

During one of his passionate services, Powell pledged four months of his salary to charity works. "Before I could finish the delivery of the sermon," he said later, "the audience was rushing forward placing money on the table 'to feed a hungry God.'" One woman left a week's wages,

The Reverend Adam Clayton Powell, Sr., pastor of Harlem's Abyssinian Baptist Church, believed religion's mission was to save people's lives as well as their souls. In one three-month period of the Great Depression, Powell's church served 28,500 free meals and gave away 525 food baskets, 2,564 pairs of shoes, and 17,928 articles of clothing.

and Powell recalled that "the trustees counted in cash and pledges twenty-five hundred dollars including my thousand dollars. It was the most impressive climax to a sermon I had ever witnessed." Powell and the Abyssinian Baptist Church continued to collect money; food, coal, kerosene, and clothes purchased from the fund drive helped get people through cold winter nights.

"The rosy enthusiasms and hopes of 1925," Alain Locke wrote in an August 1936 article that appeared

A child navigates the rickety wooden stairs to his family's unheated apartment. In the 1930s, times were hard across America, but the depression hit the nation's black communities hardest.

Wallace Thurman, once the toast of the town for such works as his play Harlem *and novel* The Blacker the Berry, *found himself adrift when the depression brought the Renaissance to a close. His last book,* Infants of the Spring, *contains this question and answer: "What is to be done about anything?" "Nothing."*

in *Survey Graphic*, "were . . . cruelly deceptive mirages." Recanting his previous claim in *The New Negro*, Locke forcefully stated, "There is no cure or saving magic in poetry and art for . . . precarious marginal employment, high mortality rates, civic neglect." Indeed, poverty struck not only the ordinary Harlemite but ended the careers of many of the period's artists as well. Once-wealthy patrons who saw their funds reduced by the depression gave up their black artist and poet protégés along with their black maids.

The production of black art did not come to a halt with the onset of the Great Depression. Publishers still printed books by black writers, and the better-known nightclubs managed to stay in business and to provide employment to black musicians. But the era of artistic opportunity was over. Smaller clubs disappeared, throwing hordes of less-famous musicians out of work. Book sales were weak, magazines folded, and black writers saw their income from royalties and article sales reduced to a pittance. More important, the second jobs, patronage, and fellowships on which most American artists relied for survival simply vanished.

During the 1930s black artists who had flocked to Harlem or to Chicago's South Side departed to wherever a secure income could be obtained, and the vibrant intellectual life of Harlem all but evaporated. Countee Cullen returned to the scene of his youth, New York City's De Witt Clinton High School, to teach French to such students as future novelist James Baldwin (who interviewed him for the school paper). One of Cullen's fellow teachers was Jessie Fauset. Arna Bontemps moved to Alabama to teach junior college; Nella Larsen became a nurse. Artists who were less educated took menial jobs. The early 1930s found Kid Ory running a chicken farm, Sidney Bechet working as a tailor, and Claude McKay working as a laborer in a welfare camp. The stress of poverty took an even greater toll on novelists Wallace Thurman and Rudolph Fisher, who died within a week of each other in 1934—Thurman in a charity ward.

Although the Great Depression effectively ended the Harlem Renaissance, it could not destroy the era's artistic, political, literary, and musical legacy. Not only are many of the renaissance's works and artists still tremendously respected and influential today, but their example and their success opened doors for generations of future black artists. In 1910, black artists had little chance for mainstream recognition, but by 1930, publishing a novel by a talented black writer or producing a record by a talented black musician was simply seen as good business. Bleak years were indeed ahead, but blacks had made more than a beginning in the quest for equality.

FURTHER READING

Anderson, Jervis. *This Was Harlem, 1900–1950*. New York: Farrar Straus Giroux, 1981.

Berendt, Joachim E. *The Jazz Book: From Ragtime to Fusion and Beyond*. Translated by H. Bredigkeit, et al. Revised edition. Brooklyn, NY: Lawrence Hill Books, 1992.

Bloom, Harold, ed. *Black American Poets and Dramatists of the Harlem Renaissance*. New York: Chelsea House, 1995.

———. *Black American Prose Writers of the Harlem Renaissance*. New York: Chelsea House, 1994.

Franklin, John Hope. *From Slavery to Freedom: A History of Negro Americans*. 5th edition. New York: Knopf, 1980.

Hughes, Langston. *The Big Sea: An Autobiography*. New York: Knopf, 1940.

Lawler, Mary. *Marcus Garvey*. New York: Chelsea House, 1988.

Marks, Carole. *Farewell, We're Good and Gone: The Great Black Migration*. Bloomington: Indiana University Press, 1989.

Osofsky, Gilbert. *Harlem: The Making of a Ghetto*. New York: Harper and Row, 1963.

Stafford, Mark. *W. E. B. Du Bois*. New York: Chelsea House, 1989.

White, Walter. *A Man Called White*. New York: Viking Press, 1948.

INDEX

KERRY CANDAELE is a professor, writer, Ph.D. candidate, and Richard Hofstadter Fellow in American History at Columbia University. He is the author of *Controversies in American History* and has written for the *Encyclopedia of African American Culture*. He teaches African-American history and other courses at Marymount Manhattan College in New York City and is presently working on a book about working-class intellectuals of the 19th century.

CLAYBORNE CARSON, senior consulting editor of the MILESTONES IN BLACK AMERICAN HISTORY series, is a professor of history at Stanford University. His first book, *In Struggle: SNCC and the Black Awakening of the 1960s* (1981), won the Frederick Jackson Turner Prize of the Organization of American Historians. He is the director of the Martin Luther King, Jr., Papers Project, which will publish 12 volumes of King's writings.

DARLENE CLARK HINE, senior consulting editor of the MILESTONES IN BLACK AMERICAN HISTORY series, is the John A. Hannah Professor of American History at Michigan State University. She is the author of numerous books and articles of black women's history, as well as the editor of the two-volume *Black Women in America: An Historical Encyclopedia* (1993). Her most recent work is a collection of essays entitled *Hine Sight: Black Women and the Re-Construction of American History*.

PICTURE CREDITS

Every effort has been made to contact the copyright owners of photographs and illustrations used in this book. In the event that the holder of a copyright has not heard from us, he or she should contact Chelsea House Publishers.

AP/Wide World Photos: p. 111; Archive Photos/Frank Driggs Collection: pp. 87, 90-91, 101, 103; the Beinecke Rare Book and Manuscript Library, Yale University: p. 114; the Bettmann Archive: pp. 32, 39, 40, 45, 99; Brown Brothers: pp. 54, 84, 89; Corbis-Bettmann: p. 18; courtesy Harlem Globetrotters: p. 75; Library of Congress: frontis, pp. 14-15, 53, 73; Lockwood Library, University of Rochester, NY: pp. 26-27; The Mariners' Museum: p. 64; National Baseball Library and Archive, Cooperstown, NY: pp. 76, 77; Photofest: pp. 66-67, 69, 70; the Schomburg Center for Research in Black Culture, the New York Public Library: pp. 20, 23, 29, 31, 56-57, 58, 62, 63, 80, 93, 95, 96, 108, 112, 113; UPI/Bettmann: pp. 28, 33, 37, 41, 42-43, 44, 46, 48, 78-79, 83; UPI/Bettmann Newsphotos: pp. 106-107; the Western Reserve Historical Society: p. 24.

DATE